STUFFED ANIMALS

A COLLECTION OF MICROFICTION

WAYNE JOHNSTON

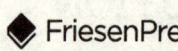 FriesenPress

One Printers Way
Altona, MB R0G 0B0
Canada

www.friesenpress.com

ISBN
978-1-03-917231-9 (Hardcover)
978-1-03-917230-2 (Paperback)
978-1-03-917232-6 (eBook)

1. LITERARY COLLECTIONS, ESSAYS

Distributed to the trade by The Ingram Book Company

BOETHIUS

I would never have found the shop if my attention had not been drawn by the clatter of a labourer dragging his barrow over the alley's cobblestones. When I looked for the source of the noise my eye caught the word "Boethius" carved over a dimly lit alcove. My curiosity could not be resisted. I opened the heavy oaken door and beheld a chaotic display of eccentric artifacts and curious devices. On one shelf I discovered vials and jars of many colours. Closer examination revealed that many of the jars contained embalmed creatures that were beyond my imagining. Another shelf featured machines of unknown purpose with many pulleys and dials. I almost lost my breath when I turned and saw a vast assortment of silken brocades. The rich hues were more luminous than the oil lamps that lined the walls. Fantastical creatures were depicted parading through mystical landscapes. My attention was finally arrested by the most unusual clock I have ever encountered. It seemed to be carved from a single block of ebony inlaid with alabaster numerals. A hinge held the crystal face behind which was an ornate minute hand and a hair-thin second hand. There was no hour hand. There was no discernable movement nor any sound that I could detect.

Then I heard the sound of a clock, but it was behind me. When I turned around I saw the ancient shopkeeper approaching. His arthritic bones were ticking and talking with each step as he hobbled toward me. His snow-white hair fell over his shoulders which were covered by a velvet cape. His face suggested a combination of wisdom and mirth. He peered through a thicket of eyebrows and introduced himself. "My name is Boethius. Welcome to my shop."

"Thank you. Where did you acquire these wonderful things you have for sale?"

"Oh, they're not for sale. Ownership is a fallacy. The land we live on, the children we cherish, the bodies we inhabit; these are fleeting privileges. We own nothing. My wares are only available for rent."

"So this clock. I'm intrigued by this clock but it seems to be broken."

"Ah, the Consolation Clock. Yes, it is broken but objects, like people, when they fall victim to age and infirmity can discover unique gifts that were hidden behind their youthful functionality. This clock, when activated, will only run for one minute. You may ask, 'what use is a clock that only runs for one minute?' Well, let me explain. Every human life is made up of sixty key moments. No more, no less. Everything else is just filler. Depending on where the minute hand is positioned the clock will present the corresponding moment from the life of the person who has activated it."

"And why is it called the 'Consolation Clock?'"

"Perhaps you are too young to appreciate this but as we go around the wheel of life we experience increasing loss and regret and sorrow. This clock offers some consolation. You have one opportunity to re-experience a moment from your past, or to discover a moment from your future. You must choose wisely. The clock can only be used once."

"I would like to rent this clock."

Boethius accepted my payment and then led me to a small room that had been concealed by heavy drapes. He placed the clock on a pedestal and then handed me an iron key with a garnet embedded in its bow.

"When you have made your decision, open the clock face and position the minute hand. Then insert the key in the clock's base. Your moment will last for one complete circuit of the second hand. Once your moment has expired, you can never use the clock again. Take your time when choosing your moment."

Alone with the clock my heart beat rapidly. It was a daunting choice. I tried to work methodically through my options. I thought about my early childhood. My father died when I was only three. I never knew him. Should I choose a moment when I might meet my father? What about my first kiss? My first love? And what of my future? What will I be doing ten years from now? And where was the present moment on this clock? Was I near the three with many years yet to live? Not everyone is granted a full life. Perhaps I am already at the nine and will die soon. The more I stewed about the choice the more obsessed I became with questions of my own demise. With trembling hand I opened the face of the clock and rotated the minute hand until it rested one minute before the twelve. Then I inserted the key.

I heard a woman's voice speaking softly to me in a reassuring tone.

"My name is Filfia. I will guide you through this moment. Try to remain calm. The light will begin to fade. Your breath will become more laboured. Your heart will stop. You will be at peace."

Despite her urging, I began to panic. What have I done? I'm not prepared to die. I struggled for breath but my lungs would not expand. I felt dizzy and confused. I felt enclosed by darkness. Then a subtle transformation began. I began to feel hopeful and at peace. As my panic subsided I heard a sound. It was a rhythmic thrumming as though I were curled in the belly of an enormous clock.

Before my time expired I called out to Filfia. "But when? I need to know when is this moment of my death?"

"Ah, don't you know? It is the moment before your birth."

AZAHAR

I can't believe I've agreed to accompany my parents on this cruise of theirs. I mean, has there ever been a worse time to travel? COVID, extreme weather events, World War III on the horizon, chaos in the travel industry. We wore masks for the entire flight. The flight to Chicago was easy but then all the way from Chicago to Rome? My God, the air quality on planes is bad enough to begin with. It would be one thing if this were a trip I actually wanted to do, but being glued to my parents while they take selfies of themselves on the deck of a cruise ship, holding up colourful drinks like they're toasting their friends back home? Tina, why did you not talk me out of this?

• • •

Of course, the airline lost my luggage. What would you expect? We have one day in Rome before we board the cruise ship. If my bag doesn't show up before then I'll be screwed.

• • •

So we're on the ship with about an hour before we leave port when I hear that my luggage has arrived. A porter brings my bag to my cabin. And, honest to God, Tina, he was so cute. Unfortunately I was wearing a top that I'd borrowed from my mom so he must think I have terrible taste in clothes. Still, I have my own clothes now and I'll be stylin' for the rest of this trip.

• • •

We just made a stop in a place called Ephesus, in Turkey. The ancient ruins are truly awe-inspiring, but I hate being shepherded around as part of a tour group. It's like when you see toddlers from a daycare walking single file with the caregivers making sure no one wanders off. You're told what to look at and what your reaction is supposed to be. It was almost enough to turn me off the place entirely. Then it went from bad to worse when my mom came out with this comment: "This is a nice place but they really need a bar here. The dust and heat make you thirsty for a tall cool one."

• • •

Tina, do you remember that porter I told you about? Well I just ran into him on the deck of the cruise ship. He was on a break and he stayed to talk with me for the longest time. His name is Azahar and he's from Yemen. Apparently, the name Azahar means the flower of an orange tree. He told me his family in Yemen owns an orchard of orange trees. I said I was shocked because I had the impression that Yemen was nothing but desert. He didn't seem offended. But then he talked about how important the orange tree is to his family, how the tree has roots in one place but the fruit and leaves can travel to distant places. Yet there is a strong sense that the members of the family are always connected and nourish each other even if they become dispersed. And, Tina, you're not going to believe this, but Azahar has a little brother in Columbus. I said, "OMG, that's where I live!" His brother was sent to the States to live with cousins to keep him safe. Azahar is working to make enough money to move there and take care of his little brother. I know you'll be laughing at me, Tina, but I think I'm in love.

• • •

The next stop on the cruise was Istanbul. I was determined not to go through another group tour experience. I told my parents I wasn't feeling well and was going to stay in my cabin. After they had left I went out to get some air and I ran into Azahar in a stairwell. He said, "I have the afternoon off. If you're willing to wait until the end of my shift, we could explore Istanbul together." And that's what we did! We went to a neighbourhood called Sultanahmet and saw architecture that was mind-blowing. We stopped into the Grand

Bazaar. It was a bit too touristy but while we were there Azahar bought a gold pendant for his little brother. It was a real orange leaf that had been dipped in gold. I think this has been the best day of my life. We were back on the ship before my parents. I couldn't stop smiling as they told me about all the things they had seen on their tour.

• • •

During dinner with my parents our waiter passed me a note. It was from Azahar saying he needed to talk to me when I was done eating. My parents were excited about the bouzouki concert slated for the after-dinner entertainment but I told them there was something I needed to do. I met Azahar on the deck. He told me that he had been assigned to another ship and that we'd be parting ways when we docked in Athens. Then he gave me the gold leaf. He said, "I want you to take this home to Columbus and give it to my brother. I'll give you his address. He'll know what it means." Tears started filling my eyes and he went on, "I will be there before long. And you will show me around your city."

• • •

We disembarked on the Faliro Pier in Athens. Azahar had to finish his shift and then would be gone by the time we returned from our day of sightseeing. I had the gold leaf around my neck and held it against my heart as my eyes scanned the lower deck. I finally spotted Azahar and we waved to each other. Tears were streaming down my face. My parents must have been wondering what was going on but I didn't care.

MAGNUS THE MAGNIFICENT

Magnus landed in the hog pen adjacent to the swine ring. His head made solid contact with the feed trough, which snapped his neck but also caused heavy bleeding out of a gaping wound in his skull. The wood of the trough split open and the blood-soaked slop seeped out, staining Magnus's jacket and pooling in the soil beneath him. Carl Turnbull's prize-winning Hampshire sow happened to be lying in the pen at the time, fast asleep, undisturbed by the sudden arrival. The way Magnus landed, curled slightly in the fetal position, it almost looked like he was mocking the sow, mirroring her position, but she took no offense. Angus Campbell was the first person into the pen to check on Magnus. He called for a few men to help him transfer Magnus out of the pen. They laid him in the grass nearby. I guess it was a more dignified spot but there were peanut shells and deflated balloons all around him so it still seemed like a bit of a joke. Someone found a horse blanket to throw over him and eventually Duncan Shire brought his buggy up so they could transport Magnus to the office of Doctor Geddes. I think everyone could tell that Magnus was beyond any help that the doctor could offer. Mothers seemed to recover from the distraction and remember their children, gaping with shock and incomprehension. The children were shepherded off to find more benign diversions.

I met Helen when we were both thirteen. Her family moved to town that summer as her father had bought the local newspaper. I didn't pay much attention to her for a few years because, like most boys that age, I was more focused on playing sports and getting into trouble than courting girls. But that eventually changed. The summer of that year, 1898 we're talking about,

I really fell for her. Of course, things back then weren't like they are now. There was only so much we could do. We'd go for walks, I'd take her for an ice cream float at Sullivan's Dairy Bar, we'd go swimming in the river, but lots of other kids would be with us. It was a big deal when I got to hold her hand. We were very naive in those days. But in my heart I felt she was the one for me, that we would eventually marry and have children of our own. So that fall she was back in school but I had to work the fields. I couldn't go back to school until after the harvest. My dad needed me and my brother at that time of year more than any other. With her in school and me working at the farm, the summer romance lost its shine. I didn't think much of it. I was sure we'd pick up where we left off once I returned to school. She was still the most beautiful girl I'd ever seen so it was never a case of losing interest. I don't think she saw it that way though.

Our farm grew sugar beets and once harvest season began we worked hard throughout every hour of daylight. There was no consideration given to taking a day off, even on the weekends, until the harvest was complete. The first stage of the work was defoliation. While the beets were still in the ground we would cut the leaves from the plants using knives called scalpers. Then we would retrace our steps, digging the bulbs out of the soil. Using a heavy hand brush we would give them an initial cleaning before collecting them in bushel baskets. The baskets would then be hauled to a waiting cart for transport back to the barn. In the barn, the beets would be sorted by weight. The beets would then be thoroughly washed and dried, then stacked in piles. This probably sounds like a simple matter but the piling of beets is actually the trickiest part. The piles could be as high as twenty feet, and the beets needed to be stacked in such a way as to ensure adequate ventilation. If not done right an entire pile could fall victim to rot. Our family's livelihood depended on getting healthy beets to market. The days were long and my back, even at my young age, ached for weeks on end. And although I wore gloves as much as possible, my hands were always stained red like those of a bloodthirsty killer. I didn't enjoy this work but it was so engrained in our yearly cycle that I never questioned its necessity.

The annual harvest could be an ordeal but it was followed every year by an event that brought joy to people of all ages: the town's fall fair. We all looked forward to this opportunity to celebrate our bounty, show off our finest produce and livestock, and mostly just to have fun. Virtually everyone in town came out to enjoy the exhibits, eat the food, and participate in the games, but many were also competitors in some part of the program. For my part, I registered that year for the hay-bale stacking event. While most of the entrants came from livestock farms I felt that I was as strong as any of them and perhaps my experience stacking beets could give me an edge. I knew that Helen would be contributing an embroidery project in the "ladies work" category. She also volunteered to be the hospitality coordinator for the fair. There was a special buzz that year because of something called "Edison's Perfected Phonograph," which was going to be demonstrated in the exhibition hall. It had also been announced that a travelling high-wire artist would be performing at our fair as part of his North American tour. He was known as "Magnus the Magnificent." As I understood it, he would traverse a cable strung between the roof of the cattle barn and the flag pole by the baseball diamond. We had all heard of such stunts being performed at Niagara Falls and in the big American cities, but to see it in our own town would be a memorable experience.

Magnus arrived two days before the fair opened so that he could oversee installation of the cable for his act. Arrangements had been made for him to billet with the Campbell family. Helen, as hospitality coordinator, met him at the train station and introduced him to Angus Campbell. People were surprised how young he was, maybe about five years older than me. But he carried himself with a level of self-assurance that I could never imitate. He had a lot more experience with the world than I'd had at that time. He had been adored in almost every major city on the continent. For my part, I had only ever been to the city once and the experience had made me feel small and insignificant. I can only imagine how Magnus's high-wire vantage point would make him feel magnificent indeed, especially when the crowds of spectators would look up and cheer him on. Frankly, from the first glimpse I got of him, I didn't like him at all.

My distaste for Magnus increased dramatically when I heard he had been spotted with Helen at Sullivan's Dairy Bar. This seemed totally inappropriate to me and an abuse of Helen's role of hospitality coordinator. When I learned of this indiscretion I dropped by to see Helen at the earliest opportunity.

"Is it true that you went to Sullivan's with this high-wire artist?"

"Yes, why? Do you have a problem with that?"

"Indeed I do and I think you should as well. Do you realize how being seen with a boy like that will damage your reputation? And how do you think it makes me feel? I thought you were my girl."

"I have to say, I've been starting to wonder. I've barely seen you since August. Besides, I really like Magnus. He's very charming and he has so many stories to tell from his travels throughout North America."

"Fine. I guess it's really none of my business."

And I left her standing on her front porch.

Back at the farmhouse I was so agitated with anger and jealousy that I couldn't settle into dinner. When dusk fell I grabbed my leather gloves and wrapped some lard in a piece of fabric and made my way to the fairgrounds. I climbed in a window of the cattle barn, scaled a ladder to the hay loft, and made my way to the roof of the barn. I approached the cable that had been installed for Magnus's act, which was due to be performed the next day. I put on my gloves, wrapped my legs around the cable, and began inching my way out. I was scared but it probably helped that I couldn't see the ground both because of the darkness and because I was hanging belly-up from the cable. When I got to about the midway point, I took out the lard and slathered it over a section of the cable. Then I slowly made my way back to the roof of the cattle barn. I can't say that I had a clear intent to commit murder. I simply wanted to bring Magnus the Magnificent down to earth.

VANITY LIZARD

I have killed my son-in-law. Frankly, it's something I've wanted to do from the moment I met him.

My daughter Kaitlin was at grad school in British Columbia. She had been planning to come home for a visit during the summer but it came as a bit of surprise when she said she was bringing someone to meet us. This signaled a serious relationship.

When I picked them up at the airport I was a bit taken aback by the size of his suitcase. They were only staying for a few days. In contrast, Kaitlin had a small duffle bag. I gave her a long embrace and then reached my hand out to her new man. He introduced himself as Philippe.

"Nice to meet you, Philippe. So, do you have French heritage?"

"Ah, no," he responded. "My name is actually Phillip, but I've been going by Philippe lately. I think it has a better ring to it."

I muttered under my breath, "Hmm, well, maybe we'll just call you Phil then, shall we?"

I followed that with a more audible, "Let's get you two home. Your mother will be eager to see you, Kaitlin. She's been busy preparing a special dinner for your return."

"Why am I not surprised?" responded Kaitlin. "And I'm sure I can guess what it will be."

When we got home, Sandra came out of the kitchen to greet us. I raised my eyebrows to signal that I wasn't so sure about this Philippe character. Sandra reacted with an admonitory scowl and brushed past me.

We sat in the living room and chatted for about an hour before Sandra announced that dinner was ready. Kaitlin helped her set the table while Philippe went upstairs with his suitcase to get changed. After the table was ready there was still no sign of Philippe so we returned to the living room. After about twenty minutes I was getting concerned that Sandra's meal would be drying out so I turned to Kaitlin and asked, "Do you think Philippe is OK? He's been gone an awfully long time."

Kailin explained, "Oh, he's fine. Philippe likes to dress for dinner. Sometimes he puts on three different outfits before he settles on the right one. He'll be down soon."

When he finally showed up he was wearing a green shirt with French cuffs and a silk paisley tie. It was at that point that I came to a firm conclusion about Philippe: I really didn't like him.

Kaitlin and Philippe were married that fall, unfortunately. I honestly couldn't see what she was drawn to. It's not so much that I expected her to share my distaste for him, but they were so different in interests and values. She seemed happy though, and, as they say, that's what really matters.

We didn't see much of them for several years after the wedding as they set up permanent residence in BC. Kaitlin was doing a post doc and Philippe managed to secure a tenure-track position with the university.

For years we had been talking to Kaitlin about taking a trip to Ghana. She had been there as a little girl when Sandra and I were doing a volunteer assignment in Accra. Kaitlin longed to return to compare reality with her hazy memories. So we all decided to finally do that trip this year. It would not only give Kaitlin a chance to see Ghana again but also provide us with some much-needed quality time together.

The flight to Accra was through Brussels. It was a long haul but uneventful. When we stepped out of the airplane on the tarmac the heat and humidity hit us like an assault. Outside the Kotoka Airport I picked a cab driver who looked trustworthy and we arrived at the hotel toward the end of the afternoon. After checking in we decided to have a drink by the pool before going to dinner. We used the time to talk about our aspirations for the week in Ghana. We decided to spend the first few days in Accra itself and then take two excursions outside the city before the week ended. The first would be a bus trip to a monkey sanctuary near Ho and the other would be a canopy walk in Kakum National Park.

As the time for dinner approached Philippe predictably excused himself to get changed. But he returned from his room abruptly looking shaken.

"There's a lizard on the vanity in our bathroom!" he exclaimed.

Sandra said, "Don't worry, Philippe. They're perfectly harmless." He didn't seem reassured.

On our first full day in Accra we opted to visit the National Museum. We spent a couple of hours there with artifacts of historical and cultural significance. While the relics were fascinating and often beautiful, the museum as a whole was in a state of disrepair. Everything was layered in dust and suffering from neglect. Kaitlin bought a hand-painted postcard from a vendor in the parking lot.

For dinner that evening we went to a restaurant that was our favourite when Sandra and I were in Ghana. It was an open-air place called The Country Kitchen that specialized in fufu served in plastic bowls. Philippe ordered fufu with goat but then didn't touch it as he was worried about getting sick from it.

Our outing the following day was to Kaneshi Market. It had a huge sprawl of stalls selling produce, meat, spices, clothing, and housewares. The meat was unsettling as raw chunks of animal flesh lay on wooden tables in the midday heat. Flies and odours filled the air and blood pooled around our feet. One of the more common sources of meat was the greater cane rat. I told Kaitlin and Philippe that when you buy it they give you a little bag of whatever was in the rat's stomach when it was killed. People use that to flavour soup.

"Lovely," Philippe commented. He looked like he was about to wretch.

When we left the market, Philippe asked if we could alter our dinner plans. "I know you wanted to return to another of your old favourites but would you mind if we ate at the hotel? I really feel the need of eating off white linen tablecloths, somewhere that I have some confidence that health and safety standards are enforced."

"That's totally fine," Sandra responded. "Actually, the food there is pretty good."

We managed to find the bus to Ho the next morning. It was at one of the chaotic bus terminals in Accra. The plan was to spend one night in Ho and get a car to the monkey sanctuary at 5:00 the next morning. Apparently you needed to be there early in the morning if you hoped to see the monkeys.

The way the buses work in Ghana is they will sit idle until every seat is filled in order to maximize the profit. The scheduled departure time is a bit of a fantasy. So we sat in the sweltering bus for two hours, waiting for it to leave. Philippe's shirt was drenched with sweat, which was making him very testy. At one point he got off the bus and bought a two-litre bottle of water. He proceeded to drink the entire thing without offering any to the rest of us. I turned in my seat and warned him, "Philippe, I just thought I should point out that there is no toilet on this bus."

The trip to Ho took three hours, which was almost as long as we'd sat waiting for the bus to depart. After about an hour Philippe started getting very agitated. He said to no one in particular, "I'm going to have to get him to stop so I can take a pee."

After working up the nerve to overcome the public shame, he called out to the driver, "Excuse me, sir. Could you please stop? I need to go to the washroom."

The driver looked at him incredulously in the rearview mirror. Of course, in Ghana, the word washroom refers to a laundry.

Philippe, getting desperate, determined to be more explicit. "I need to urinate!"

A local woman leaned across the aisle, touched his forearm and explained, "The bus will be stopping at a rest area soon."

Philippe was very relieved and thanked her; however, "soon" turned out to be a relative term. When the bus finally pulled over, Philippe bolted down the aisle, discarding any courtesy to the other passengers who wanted to get off. The rest area was merely a ditch with a metre-high wall to offer a suggestion of privacy. Philippe released a steady stream that seemed to last for five minutes. He returned to the bus embarrassed but feeling like he was emotionally better equipped for the adventure ahead.

As planned, we all got up early enough to meet the driver at 5:00 a.m., to take us to the monkey sanctuary. The hour-long drive was harrowing. In the pre-dawn darkness, the car careened down the road, rattling and creaking as the driver made a half-hearted attempt to avoid the women who walked the roadside to take their produce to the nearest market. At one point I discerned two dark shapes in the middle of the road that didn't encourage the driver to slow down at all. I assumed they must have been bags of garbage but as we slipped between them I saw that they were actually goats.

At the sanctuary we were encouraged to buy bananas to coax the monkeys out of the forest. Sure enough, they appeared in no time, grabbed the bananas with an air of entitlement, and disappeared again. Philippe griped, "We came all this way for that?"

Philippe insisted that he would not take another intercity bus so when the day came to visit Kakum National Park, we hired a private driver. Despite seatbelts that didn't work and a cracked windshield, it did provide a more civilized experience.

The forest environment offered the first real respite from the heat that we'd experienced that week. It was clearly a highlight for Kaitlin as she enthused about the variety of trees, plants, butterflies, and birds. She must have taken a thousand photographs. The canopy walk itself was thrilling, if a little precarious.

About mid-way along the 350-metre walk I heard Philippe complain, "I can walk the Capilano Suspension Bridge back in North Vancouver. I didn't have to travel to the other side of the world for this."

I was focused on recording a brief video with my phone. I wanted to capture the swaying of the structure high above the forest floor. All my attention was on filming when I collided with Philippe. I must have caught him when he was slightly off balance because he took a header over the rope restraint. As I watched him fall to his demise, I felt uneasy because the walkway was now swaying more dramatically.

DANI ININI

You are cordially invited to attend the wedding of Princeton Paisley and Monica Gamillah. The wedding will span four days, from August 21 through August 24. We will be gathering at the remote luxury resort of Dani Inini Lodge, on Lake Maminaadizi. Upon receipt of your RSVP, arrangements will be made for a charter flight to take you and a guest to the lodge on August 20. Once you are there, everything will be provided for your stay. You will not lack for diversion as we have hired numerous musical acts, including an unprecedented private concert by the legendary Robbie Robertson. This will be an experience none of us will ever forget. Please let us know that you will be attending to help Princeton and Monica celebrate this momentous occasion.

Terry was thrilled when she received the invitation back in February. She had never been to the far north, but having been to Princeton's home on the Bridle Path she had no doubt that it would be an opulent and decadent experience from beginning to end. And with any party thrown by Princeton, half of the excitement was seeing who would show up. Models, actors, artists, political dignitaries. She felt giddy with anticipation.

The wedding was only a week away and she decided, at this relatively late date, that she needed a new dress for the trip. She would need to bring at least eight different outfits to see her through the four days. She took the elevator down to the parking garage of her lakeshore condo where her Lexus was parked. As she pulled out past the encampment of homeless Native people living under the Gardiner Expressway, she cringed. Their numbers seemed to increase each day. She considered it an eyesore and worried that it could devalue property values in the area.

Terry drove to her favourite shop in Rosedale. After trying on several dresses, she selected a black Givenchy dress that the shop had just received from Italy. "This is from the 2022 collection, which is creating quite a stir," the shopkeeper told her. Terry thought immediately of her enamel brooch with the native motif and knew it would look stunning on this dress.

Back at her parking garage she was getting out of her car with her new purchase when someone shoved her violently into the side of the car. Her face hit the door jamb and she came down heavily on her knee. By the time she collected herself the assailant had disappeared along with her $600 dress.

Badly shaken, Terry returned to her condo unit. She determined that her injuries didn't warrant a trip to the hospital, although it was clear her cheek would be swollen and bruised. She considered calling the police, but, given that she hadn't got even a glimpse of her attacker, she decided that wouldn't be worth the aggravation. Instead, she called her city councillor, whom she had met at one of Princeton's parties.

"Richard, you have got to do something about those god-damned Indians living under the Gardiner. One of them just attacked me in my parking garage."

The councillor promised to do what he could but also convinced Terry to report the incident to the police.

On August 20, Terry took a limo to the airport. As the vehicle took the ramp to the Gardiner, she peered at the Native encampment. She half-expected to see her Givenchy dress flying like a flag but all she saw was the usual array of cardboard boxes and sleeping bags.

The wedding was everything Terry had hoped it would be. The food was delicious, the accommodations were first class, and there was no shortage of fascinating people to meet. There was almost always live music in the main lounge area, including bands brought in from Montreal and San Francisco. Because of the northern setting, Princeton and Monica thought it would be fun to incorporate some Native themes into the experience. One evening they staged a theatrical pow wow. Some of the guests, after drinking most of the day, joined in with mock Native singing, like fans at an Atlanta Braves baseball game.

People were constantly asking Terry about the bruising on her face, which made her almost unrecognizable. With each telling of the story she made it both more dramatic and more humorous. It evolved from a tale of personal trauma into something more like a scene from a slapstick movie.

By way of wedding favours every guest received an eagle feather. Terry quipped that an eagle must have been plucked clean for them to come up with so many feathers. "It takes the term 'bald eagle' to a whole new level."

On the limo back home from her trip, descending the ramp from the Gardiner, Terry was elated to see that every trace of the Native encampment was gone. She couldn't see so much as a shred of cardboard. Upon entering her condo she found voice mail from the police. The man who had assaulted her had been arrested and her Givenchy dress had been recovered. It turned out he wasn't from the community living under the Gardiner at all. He was a laid-off software engineer living in one of the neighbouring condo towers.

Terry went into her bathroom to check on the status of her injuries. The bruising on her face was as unsightly as ever.

DISCLOSURE

I am at my brother's trial. There is something about seeing him isolated in this formal and hostile environment that makes him seem smaller and more vulnerable. I wish I could take him home and tell him everything will be OK. It's like I'm seeing him as the child I used to know.

Tim used to love building forts and castles out of cardboard boxes, cushions, and blankets. Unlike other kids Tim would build his structure and then stay quietly hidden inside for hours. It wasn't unusual for the family to see a full morning or afternoon go by and realize we hadn't seen Tim since breakfast or lunch.

When other kids in our neighbourhood went to summer camp to swim, canoe, play sports, make friends, and sing songs around a campfire, Tim adamantly refused to go. He preferred to stay home alone and watch old movies in the basement of our parents' house. I think he needed an environment that gave him a sense of control. The more he had to share space with other people, the less he was able to cope.

Of course, it didn't help that he was always socially awkward. Kids pick up on that from a young age and the response can be ruthless. He often came home complaining about teasing and mocking and at times he was bloodied and teary after being beaten up by other boys.

Tim always seemed most at peace with himself when he was forced to be in seclusion for a period of time. For example, he suffered a torn ACL when he was about twenty years old. He spent a couple of weeks back at our parents' house during his initial recovery. I was struck by how calm and self-assured he seemed during that period, despite the physical discomfort. I remember one visit in particular when I came over to watch a football game with him. Tim was stretched out on a La-Z-Boy recliner. The announcer was talking about a recently retired player who left the spotlight to live alone in a cabin in Alaska. Tim's eyes seemed to sparkle when he expressed admiration for that choice of lifestyle.

The crown attorney makes reference to Tim's prior conviction for assault. I remember this incident well since it happened at my house. Tim had been living in my basement and my wife and I were getting concerned about him as he seemed increasingly unwilling to leave the house. He wasn't causing us any grief to speak of, but we worried about his mental health and whether he would ever get his life on track. There was a group of friends from his high school days who were concerned about him as well. I honestly believe they were thinking of his well-being when they came over that night.

Four of these old high school buddies showed up at the house with a six-pack of beer. They were downstairs for a while drinking and listening to music. As I understand, they were determined to get Tim out of the house. They felt that a night on the town might be the key to restoring his ability to cope in the world. I went downstairs when the shouting began to alarm me. These friends were clearly over-reacting in their zeal to save Tim. They grabbed him by the arms and were trying to force him out the door. Tim became increasingly panicked and, before I could intervene, he pulled a small knife out of his back pocket and stabbed one of his friends. It wasn't enough to do any real harm, but Tim was charged with assault and it severed the only social ties he seemed to have at that time. Although he'd always been an introvert, this new period of social isolation seemed to diminish his ability to relate to people. He was spending too much time online, entrenched in dis-concerting fringe communities. His substance abuse problems also deepened.

While it wasn't uncommon for us to go a week without talking to Tim, we were at least aware of his comings and goings. Then there was a patch of time in the winter when Tim didn't go outside at all. We could tell from the undisturbed snow that he hadn't used the door to his apartment. There was a door to the basement inside that we kept locked out of respect for Tim's privacy but I eventually became so concerned that I went down to check on him. The basement was never very bright but Tim had put blankets in the windows to block all light from coming in. I was struck by the stale smell of neglect. I found him sitting on the floor behind his sofa. When I asked him if he was OK, he had a response that I found bizarre and unnerving. He said he had decided to spend a period of time completely cut off from the world. He explained, "There's been something happening in my head and I needed to understand it. I've wanted to eliminate all external distractions so I could just focus on that. I feel like I've gone deeper into my soul than I've ever been."

"Well, that sounds like a true spiritual journey, bro. I hope I didn't disrupt you by coming down here."

"No, that's OK. I've done what I needed to do. Besides, the garbage is going a bit maggoty so it's about time I rejoin the outside world."

It was shortly after that that he started mentioning a guy named Derek. I guess he connected with him either through social media or his need for illicit substances or both. Derek started coming around to see Tim and, in stark contrast to his home confinement, Tim was spending a lot of time away from home. Based on what we saw of Derek we were pretty sure he was a dealer. He certainly looked the part. He rode a motorcycle and was covered in tattoos. Tim seemed eager to win Derek's approval. I'm sure Derek was behind Tim's ill-fated decision to commit armed robbery at the convenience store. I can't see him doing something so reckless, otherwise.

As much as Tim was motivated by winning Derek's approval, I think the draw was really more Derek's girlfriend, Aidan. He seemed to be obsessed with her. He followed her on social media and talked about her as some sort of ethereal angel. I struggled to understand how someone so heavenly would tie herself to a lowlife like Derek. I'm sure she had her flaws but Tim seemed blind to them. The only time I ever met her was when Derek and Aidan dropped by to see Tim. Clearly there was some sort of transaction that Derek was eager to discuss but my presence forced him to be discreet. They stayed for a beer in the backyard. The entire time Tim gazed at Aidan like she was a miracle personified. It's hard to imagine that Derek didn't pick up on Tim's doting attention. Maybe he just didn't care because he knew Tim was no threat.

Given that Tim never had any money I was stunned when I heard he had spent $200 on a kniffe. I suspect he was skipping meals in order to save up for that knife as I had never seen him so thin. He had taken a bus to Toronto to buy the knife directly from a collector there. Apparently it was a traditional knife from Nepal know as a *khukuri*, used by Ghurka warriors and hunters. I'll admit it was an impressive piece of craftsmanship. I wouldn't have been surprised to see it in a display case at the Royal Ontario Museum.

That knife embodied whatever self-esteem Tim possessed. When I would visit Tim, the knife was always on display and often Tim would handle it, polish it, and caress it during our conversations. I think it made him feel unique and maybe a little dangerous. It was probably the most beautiful and valuable thing he ever owned.

The crown attorney is reading from the transcript of Tim's confession while Tim gazes at him as though he's not sure what he will hear.

"I stood at the side of the store waiting until I was sure there was no one around. Then I put the nylon stocking over my head and entered the store. I had my *khukuri* knife in my hand. The door had a bell that rang when I entered but I couldn't see a store clerk anywhere. I ran toward the stockroom at the back of the store because I thought the clerk must be there. When I got there I saw a young woman inside the milk fridge, trying to close the door. I assume she thought she'd be safe from me if she were locked in the fridge. I stuck my leg against the door to prevent her from closing it. I stepped in and thrust my knife into her stomach. I drew the knife along her throat. Then I sat down with her."

When the police arrived there was so much blood they initially thought there were two victims.

Since Tim entered a guilty plea, the trial didn't take long. As they led him out of the courtroom he looked over his shoulder and smiled at me.

MORE BODIES

My name is Jojo Bopha. I own a small restaurant in Ba Phnum that specializes in satay. I have had a good life here, but the killing has come to our province and I must escape. My plan is to travel like a wild animal, at night when it is harder to be seen. During the daylight I will sleep. There is an ancient monastery that can be reached in a couple of days. I can shelter there until I continue on to the border.

I gather together some food: nuts, dried fruit, cured meat. Then, almost as an afterthought, I take one of the larger metal skewers from my kitchen. Carrying much more than these few items would draw suspicion.

I walk down the dirt road heading south. My pace is deliberately slow at first as I pause to admire a large beng tree. I do not want to appear to be in any hurry. Labourers pass me on bicycles. There is nothing unusual, nothing to draw attention. I walk more quickly when I reach the edge of town. Rice paddies cover the land on both sides of the road. I begin to feel self-conscious, as there is no reason for a woman like me to be in the countryside at this hour of the night. I need to leave the road at the first opportunity.

I arrive at a point where there is a trail between the rice paddies. There is little chance of encountering anyone on the trail. After about half an hour, my step is interrupted by something on the path. I stumble over it and land in the shallow water of a rice paddy. In the dim moonlight I am able to recognize it as the body of a young man. My shock turns to panic as I start seeing more bodies half-submerged in the water around me. I pick myself up and resume my trek with an elevated sense of urgency.

Eventually, the trail crosses another dirt road and I decide to take that as walking is easier than on the paths. As I round a bend I see a Jeep parked under a copse of mahogany trees. I decide to take my chances with whoever I might encounter rather than reversing my course, but first I secure the skewer in the sleeve of my jacket. As I approach, I see that a soldier is dozing in the Jeep, but, before I can reconsider my options, he awakens and gets out of the Jeep with his rifle.

"What have we here? Just the thing to relieve my boredom." The soldier stands with his feet spread wide apart and his gun pointing at me.

I plead with him to let me pass, but he is in no mood to show mercy. Then I decide to bargain for my safe passage.

"Sir, I am a businesswoman. I know how to make an attractive offer. I have food that I can share with you. I can also offer you the pleasures of my body."

He responds with a smile that I find revolting. "Well, as a businesswoman, you will understand that I can't agree to a transaction without first inspecting the merchandise."

He approaches me and begins to loosen my jacket. I let the skewer slide into my hand and then plunge it through his thigh. When he falls to the ground in agony, I grab his rifle. My priority is that he won't use the rifle on me or any other innocent civilians and so I toss it across the rice paddies.

"Sir, I have killed many chickens and pigs in my time. I could easily kill you if I chose to do so."

I then wrench the skewer from his leg as I may have further use for it.

Forgoing the road I continue south on the paths. Progress will be slower going and I find it harder to keep my bearings but I feel too exposed on the roads after that encounter with the soldier. I want to be sure he can't recover and follow me in his Jeep. Out in the rice paddies there are more bodies. In fact, the farther I walk, the more numerous they become. I'm not sure what to make of that. Is the army killing labourers while they work? Or do they bring the bodies to these remote areas so they needn't bother burying them? Or perhaps there are increasing numbers making their way, like me, toward the border.

At one point I come upon a fox tearing flesh from the body of a young woman. It disturbs me so much that I run splashing through the paddies to scare it off. No doubt it will return as soon as I move on, but I can't bear to watch the desecration of the poor woman's body. That incident disorients me and I realize after about an hour that I have been walking in the wrong direction. That was precious lost time that could cost me my life.

Eventually, the sky begins to lighten and I realize I need to find a sheltered spot to wait out the daytime. In short order, I find a forest of jackfruit and bamboo that will provide both shade and concealment. I take shelter there and consume some of my food.

I fall asleep against the base of a tree. I don't know how long I have slept but I awaken with a start. Silhouetted against the harsh light are two figures looming over me. A male voice speaks.

"Look what's growing here. I would say it's ready for harvesting."

BÀTA TAIBHSE

Chelsea turned off her computer and put on her jacket. Before leaving her office, she checked her hair in the small mirror on the bookshelf. It was a habit that might suggest vanity but it had more to do with projecting a persona. She liked photos of herself taken at a dramatic angle with her hair falling over one eye. Or photos of her with a sleeveless top showing off her tattoos. She didn't want to relinquish the counter-culture identity that had come so easily in her youth.

Chelsea left her office and made her way out of the building. She walked to the locks where she could cross the canal, then down along the path by the lake to Little Italy, where she lived. It was one of those September days that seemed unwilling to surrender the warmth of summer. Many people were strolling or playing Frisbee in the park. A number of boats were out on the lake.

She decided to stop for a drink at a sidewalk patio on Preston before going home. She took a table half-hidden by a potted plant hoping to signal that she was not there to talk to people. She ordered a single malt and then pulled from her briefcase a research proposal she had to assess. Her grad students in the Scottish studies program were required to submit a plan for research that would lead to a term paper. She was meeting with this particular student the next morning so she had to be prepared to discuss his proposal.

The student's name was Duncan McPhee, and his proposal was to analyze the impact of a sculptors' guild based in Dundee in the eighteenth century. According to Duncan's proposal, this guild was responsible for introducing many Scottish artisans to the technology of lost wax casting. Also known by the French term *cire-perdue*, this process involves using a hollow wax model to make a plaster mould. The wax is then melted out and replaced with molten

31

metal. Duncan's concept was very intriguing to Chelsea. She felt it could be a valuable piece of scholarship but she had grave concerns about the proposal itself. She was not aware of anything like this in the published literature and Duncan had not provided a bibliography, which was a required component of these proposals. She was eager to address these concerns with Duncan the next morning.

By the time Chelsea left the bar she was feeling buoyed by the alcohol and somewhat distracted by Duncan's proposal. It was only a ten-minute walk to her home, but after walking for thirty minutes she realized she was in an unfamiliar neighbourhood. She couldn't imagine how she had managed to get lost on such a short walk. She decided to pick a direction and walk until she hit a familiar street. When she reached Somerset, she was able to orient herself and head home. When she arrived on her front porch she couldn't find her key. She was panicked and angry with herself. Could she have left it at the bar? Might she have dropped it somewhere on her walk? She finally found it in her jacket pocket. She never put her key in her jacket pocket.

During her walk to work the next morning, Chelsea observed that the leaves were already changing colour. She thought about how she loved the fall when the leaves are brilliant gold and crimson and amber. The beauty is short lived, as all beauty seems to be. But the loss makes way for the new green leaves of spring, which fill her with a sense of potential for the coming year.

The concept of new beginnings brought her thoughts around to her position at the university and the nagging belief that she owed it to herself to quit and launch into something new before she was too old for such bold moves. Thoughts of her younger self plagued her. Would that younger Chelsea be proud of what she'd done with her life? Had she been seduced by the security of tenure and the comfort of the familiar?

Seated at her desk in her office, Chelsea looked out the window at the empty plaza, knowing it wouldn't be empty for long. She steeled herself for the inundation of students. It was pretty much a steady stream of anxiety as they complained about impossible workloads, unreasonable deadlines, and an array of non-scholarly factors like ailing parents, noisy housemates, and failing relationships. One girl actually confessed to losing her virginity as a factor in her request for an extension. Chelsea tried to be sympathetic and supportive to all the students without actually compromising on the academic standards.

By the time she met with Duncan McPhee, she was pleased to have the opportunity for a more substantive conversation. She explained how interested she was in his proposal but that she had to confront him with her concerns.

"Let's start by talking about your interest in this guild. What is it that made you want to focus on them?"

"Well, I guess it is because we took an ancient, time-honoured technology and made it innovative in a way that had an impact throughout Scotland."

"I'm sorry, Duncan, but referring to the guild you said 'we.'"

"Did I? I'm sorry. I didn't mean to. Of course I meant to say 'they.' They were a very creative and dedicated group of artists. They built their own foundry for creating molten bronze with temperatures reaching 1,700 degrees Fahrenheit. They then trained other artisans in the region so that their expertise became widespread."

"But can you tell me where you got your information? You haven't cited any published sources. Is this proposal based on archival records?"

Duncan met her question with a steady gaze that wasn't aggressive or defensive. He seemed fully engaged and somewhat bemused. "Everything I know I learned directly from Calum MacDonnell."

"I don't know the name Calum MacDonnell. Is he a scholar at another university?"

"No, just someone I used to know."

"Well, I'm sorry, Duncan, but your research needs to have a basis in published scholarship. If you are unable to provide a proper bibliography, I won't be able to approve your project."

As she handed his proposal back to Duncan, she saw that his hands were calloused and scarred from burns. He gave her a warm smile before leaving, without indicating one way or another how he intended to respond to her criticism.

Chelsea logged into the registrar's directory and was dismayed to learn that there was no student by the name Duncan McPhee. She then walked down the hall to the office of the department head, who conducted a screening interview for every student admitted to the program. She asked him about Duncan but he assured her that no one fitting that description had been admitted.

Finally, Chelsea started searching online for the name Calum MacDonnell. It took a while but she eventually found a reference to a sculptor of that name active in Dundee in the period 1760 to 1780.

On her walk home that evening, Chelsea had to wait for a boat to pass through the locks. She sat by the footbridge over the canal and watched the water level slowly descend. As she gazed into the water in the chamber she saw a largemouth bass swimming around the boat awaiting passage. She imagined the fish being confused by its enclosure and perhaps distressed about the diminishing volume of water. When enough water was lost to match the level of the canal, the gate was opened. Chelsea watched the fish slip through on its way to the lake. As the boat followed, she saw printed on the stern the name "Bàta Taibhse," which she recognized as Gaelic for "ghost ship."

SUNNYSIDE

I spent my days working in a room barely big enough to accommodate a small desk. Seated at my computer, I could look through venetian blinds at a gravel parking lot, a patch of weeds, and a chain-link fence. To the north was a repertory cinema where I first saw *Repo Man*; to the east was the coffee shop where I got a coffee and a seed square every morning; to the south was the elementary school that my son, Ben, attended; and to the west was a residential neighbourhood where we used to rent a house. The block where my office was has since been replaced by a super pharmacy. They call the area Old Ottawa South.

After renting a house in that neighbourhood for a few years, we bought a house farther east on the Rideau River. It was the fourth house we'd lived in together but the first one we had owned. It had seemed like a promise of stability and happiness at the time.

When we made plans to separate, we settled on the date February 1. We wanted Ben to have one last family Christmas and January 1 would have been too abrupt. The plan was for me to spend a month in Toronto as a trial separation.

Although we had talked to Ben numerous times about the separation, I don't think he truly absorbed it. He might have been concerned immediately after one of our conversations but then life would seem to carry on as always. And, of course, it was all too easy to be distracted by the events of daily life so as to avoid the fact that we were surrendering hope for our relationship. I'm sure Ben understood in concept that his parents had plans to separate but he had no way to appreciate how his life would be altered.

So on February 1 I made Ben's lunch and drove him to school as I had done every other day. He could tell something was different, not the way it was meant to be, but he didn't know or didn't remember what the difference was. When I pulled up at the school I tried to wish him a good day but my throat was constricted as I fought back tears. He seemed truly mystified. He kept repeating, "What's going on? What's going on?" Then he grabbed his backpack and got out of the car. He entered the school without looking back at me.

I didn't plan on taking much with me to Toronto because at that time the concept of a temporary, trial separation still seemed believable. I thought I might be back in a month to resume where we left off. Or, better yet, with a fresh beginning. As it turned out, I retrieved my belongings some months later. My books had been tossed in the garden shed and many of them were unsalvageable.

At the end of the month in Toronto I moved back to Ottawa, taking a place in a rooming house. The idea for my return to Ottawa was that we could talk and reach an understanding about the future of our relationship. In reality, we both knew it was over and there wasn't anything to talk about.

The rooming house was a townhouse in Alta Vista. About half a dozen men were living there, each having a bedroom and sharing use of the kitchen and bathroom. I often came and went without seeing anyone, but when I did see one of the other residents, I was often hit up for money. I was something of an anomaly, having regular employment. The other men were either unemployed or casual labourers. The woman who owned the place lived in another unit in the same complex. She seemed to be mystified by my presence there. I could have afforded better accommodations but that arrangement seemed to fit with the transition my life was going through. It was a way station.

It was an emotionally volatile time for me, splitting my time between my meagre office and my meagre residence while my wife and son were nearby in the house where we had lived together. I had lost my family, my home, and my self-respect and the sadness was made worse by the proximity of all that I longed for. The separation was easier to deal with when I was living in Toronto, away from the constant reminders, away from the notion that taking a different route could lead me home, where I surely belonged. On one occasion I left my office in the middle of the morning and went to a nearby phone booth to call an old friend. The moment I heard his voice, the grief overwhelmed me and I hung up, sobbing, unable to talk.

Like any daily activity, my somnambulant arrival at the office each day lacked significance or variation. Entering through the front door, turning right at the reception desk, walking down the hall past the washroom, fishing the key out of my pocket as I turned down the next hallway to the left. My thoughts would shift to what my immediate tasks would be after my computer booted up. On one occasion, as I positioned the key to unlock my office door, I was jarred by incomprehension. The cheap plywood door was splintered. The door jamb had been torn off. Someone had broken into my office. The pattern had been fractured.

CASSIOPEIA

It was possible to detect a streetlight outside but the curtains were thick enough that the room was not illuminated. More light crept in under the door but only enough to serve as a point of orientation. Dani knew the placement of every object in her room, so there was rarely a need to have lights on.

She easily located the small safe in her closet and didn't even need to see in order to punch in the combination. Once she had it open she could identify each object by touch. She took out her MP3 player. The other objects in her safe were all sacred relics, such as the onyx pendant given to her by her grandmother. The MP3 player, on the other hand, was in the safe just to keep it out of the hands of her younger brother. He wasn't even interested in music; he was just fascinated with gadgets of any type.

She lay back on her bed, put the ear buds in, and initiated the random play. Joni Mitchell sang, "Every picture has its shadows/And it has some source of light/Blindness, blindness and sight."

She felt guilty for not listening to rap. By listening to old music from white performers it seemed as though she were betraying both her race and her generation. The fact was that she didn't connect with any of the preconceptions people had about her. She didn't like the television shows that people assumed she would watch. Other kids expected her to be into fashion, but she felt most comfortable dressing in jeans and T-shirts. Teachers encouraged her to take music and drama, but she was more interested in math and science.

Dani was glad that the next day was the first day back at school. She always did well in her classes and she enjoyed the social aspect of student life. She found the walk to school that morning to be exciting. After a summer of quiet streets there seemed to be hordes of kids giddy with anticipation. There were faces she recognized while others were clearly new to the area. She was distracted by all the stimulation and twisted her ankle by stepping on the edge of the sidewalk. She lurched forward and collided with a girl named Lori, whom she had always admired but had never really met. Lori grabbed her to prevent her from tumbling into the street. "Are you OK, girl?"

Dani clung to her longer than was necessary. "Ya, sorry about that."

"You're in Grade 10, right? I remember you from last year."

"I don't think we had any classes together but I saw you around. In the halls, in the cafeteria, and stuff."

They talked throughout the twenty-minute walk to school. Just before entering the school, Lori invited her to a party at her place Friday after school. "My mom is away for the weekend so she won't be around. You seem like a good girl but, believe me, you won't be a good girl after one of my parties."

Dani was apprehensive when she arrived at Lori's house. She had never been to a house party and this was definitely outside her comfort zone. She had elevated expectations of loud music, drinking, drugs, every room crowded with people far cooler than her. After Lori greeted her with a hug, Dani was surprised to find only half a dozen girls sitting in the living room, drinking orange sodas. There was no sign of drugs and in their place were large bowls of potato chips and cheese puffs. A lot of the conversation focused on a Japanese video game they all seemed to be obsessed with. Dani wasn't familiar with it so she felt lost but she tried to look enthusiastic. One of the girls seemed a bit full of herself but otherwise they were all very pleasant. Lori's mom had left frozen pizzas for the party, so they made those for dinner. By 8:00, the girls were leaving. As Lori said goodbye to the last of them, she asked Dani if she'd like to stay for a tour of the house. She led Dani by the hand from room to room with a constant banter of clever stories, mostly making fun of her family members. They ended up in Lori's bedroom. After intro-ducing Dani to the stuffed toys left over from her childhood, Lori turned off the light in the bedroom. She gently eased Dani onto her bed. Dani felt delirious and elated. She could not get enough of Lori's tongue in her mouth. She had never been touched in that way before. She wanted to be there in Lori's darkness forever.

[None of these events at Lori's house actually happened.]

When Dani got to school she saw that there were tables set up in the main hallway, promoting various clubs that students could join. There was one for table tennis, one for debating, one for Christian fellowship. She was immediately drawn to the Environmental Club. They had a poster showing mountains of land waste, catastrophic storms, and starving polar bears. The girl and boy behind the table explained how the club was focused on raising awareness in the local community. They said they would love to welcome Dani to their monthly after-school meetings.

The Environmental Club organized an unplugged, no-energy concert in the school gymnasium. They made arrangements for all the lights in the school to be off for the duration of the concert. About 200 kids from the school showed up and the local newspaper even reported on it. About ten musicians were scheduled to perform. There was some discussion of setting up a stage for the performances, but it was pointed out that the purpose of a stage is to enable the audience to see the artists. Since that wouldn't be possible in the darkened gym, the musicians were scattered throughout the gym, sitting on the floor with all the other kids. Dani volunteered to sing one of her favourite Joni Mitchell songs. "They took all the trees put 'em in a tree museum/And they charged the people a dollar and a half just to see 'em." She wasn't a very good singer, but since no one could see her she didn't feel as self-conscious as she otherwise might.

[There was never a concert in the dark as is described here.]

Dani entered her first class with a happy glow. The school year had barely started and she felt like her world was already expanding. New friends, new causes, new knowledge to match her bright, new back-to-school clothes. Even the smell of the teacher's cologne, which would come to repulse her, suggested new possibilities simply by its novelty. Her dad never used anything other than Aqua Velva.

The teacher gave an overview of what they would be studying that semester. He also distributed a list of novels and said everyone in the class had to pick one to read and compose a critical review. Accompanying each title was an overview of the significance of the novel. Something about the description of a novel by Joseph Conrad so intrigued Dani that she went to the school library right after class and signed it out.

At the end of the afternoon as she was leaving school, Dani opted to take an alternate route home. There was a trail along the river she had walked many times over the summer months. Along one bend in the river was a large rock where she liked to sit and watch the ducks dabbling. She decided she would sit there for a while and get a start reading her book.

The trail meandered through an old-growth woodland of maples and beeches. Dani entered the trail, savouring the solitude after a day of over-stimulation. After a while she got an uneasy sense that someone was following her. Whenever she turned to look she saw a figure step off the trail behind a tree.

Dani settled herself on the rock and took the book from her backpack. In no time at all she was so absorbed in the book that she was oblivious to the sounds around her. Otherwise, she would have heard him approaching. Suddenly, fabric was pulled over Dani's head and drawn tight at her throat. She was immediately aware of the odour of the fabric, like a shirt that hadn't been laundered in far too long. The man wound duct tape around her neck to secure the fabric, warning her not to scream or he would use his knife to silence her. He wrenched her off the rock and then pulled her stumbling down the embankment toward the river. Once there, he threw her to the ground and fell on top of her. He lifted her shirt and began pawing her breasts. Then, as quickly as the attack had started, he stood up and Dani listened to him scampering through the forest. She assumed someone must have been approaching on the trail and that he had been scared off. She tried to calm her breathing so that she could hear better what was happening. She heard the river lapping against rocks along the river's shore. She heard ducks quacking comically in the distance. She realized that her ankle was injured. She must have sprained it during the struggle. For the moment, she lay in the darkness of her rancid hood, waiting to see what would happen next.

[No assault took place in the forest.]

Growing increasingly uneasy, she decided to leave the trail, cutting through the trees to get into the adjacent neighbourhood as quickly as possible. She felt much safer on a well-lit street bordered by modest bungalows.

When Dani got home her dad asked her to plant the crocus bulbs she'd failed to get to on the weekend. She dug holes in the cool soil, placed the bulbs in the holes, and then covered them with manure compost. She thought the compost would be offensive but she actually liked the earthy aroma and the rich, dark colour. By the time she was done she had managed to get soil on the clothes she had carefully selected for her first day of school. Only then did it occur to her that she should have changed before working on the crocuses.

After dinner, Dani felt drawn back out to the garden. She stood in the darkness looking up at the stars, remembering how her grandmother had taught her to recognize the constellations. She looked up at Cassiopeia.

SIGNALS AND NOISE

The closed-circuit security camera captures Susan Moore entering the hospital at 9:41 a.m., on Tuesday, February 4. She is wearing a charcoal grey dress coat, knee-high leather boots, and a red beret. The monitor next to the camera mirrors Susan's steps but is stripped of the sense of urgency.

Susan has come to the hospital to meet her daughter Brianna in the neurology ward. Brianna has been experiencing worrisome symptoms, including double vision and headaches. Susan has been searching the web to match Brianna's symptoms to possible causes. Her worst fear is that it could be a brain tumour. Brianna's father died of brain cancer and so there is concern about a hereditary predisposition.

Based on the initial screening, Brianna is admitted to the hospital for further tests and observation. The nurses immediately take a blood sample for analysis. An MRI is scheduled as well as a CT scan. Susan stays with Brianna until the end of visiting hours and promises to return first thing the next morning.

• • •

Jeffrey has been an orderly at the hospital for over twenty years. He took the job immediately after dropping out of university and, although he's hated every workday since then, the pay is more than he could expect to make in any other job, so he has stuck it out.

Jeffrey spots Susan on her way out of the hospital. Although it has been many years, Jeffrey recognizes her from his university days. They met in a psychology class and Jeffrey was immediately attracted to her. They went on one date to a jazz club in a seedy part of the city. Things seemed to go well and Jeffrey accompanied Susan back to her apartment. Once there, Jeffrey tried to get physical with her, but everything he did seemed clumsy. Whatever rapport they had established quickly evaporated. Susan eventually asked him to leave. Jeffrey left but not before taking Susan's scarf as a memento.

Jeffrey had reached out to Susan several times after that, but she never returned his calls. It was around that time that he grew dispirited with university and quit. At the end of that academic year, Susan moved on to graduate school in Montreal.

• • •

The more time Susan spends on the internet the more theories she adds to the list of possible explanations for Brianna's symptoms. One site blames migrant workers from Mexico for Guillain-Barré syndrome. A report on the site details how a healthy young woman working at a greenhouse in Kent County contracted the disease from a Mexican coworker. She quickly became so ill that she lost the ability to walk. Susan recalls that Brianna mentioned meeting someone who spoke Spanish, but Susan couldn't recall hearing where that person was from.

Another site asserted that multiple sclerosis could be triggered by going through a metal detector. Susan's father-in-law had developed MS as a young man. By the time Susan met him he was confined to a wheelchair, could not feed himself, and was hard to understand when he spoke. He eventually died of pneumonia, when his lungs were no longer strong enough to sustain him.

Yet another site provided evidence that wind turbines increase the likelihood of suffering a stroke. There is a wind farm just outside the city. Susan tries to determine what distance from the wind turbines is considered safe but she is unable to find that information. She is reminded of an old high school friend who had a stroke that left him with only one usable arm and facial paralysis that made him too self-conscious to be out in public.

Susan finds a compelling article on Facebook that proves that cellphone use is directly linked to brain tumours. She herself has always been suspicious of cellphones and tries to limit use to only when it is absolutely necessary. Susan realized that Brianna spent an inordinate amount of time on her cellphone and wished she had done more to limit her use. She starts feeling overwhelmed with guilt for her neglect.

• • •

The first time Jeffrey sees Brianna at the hospital he experiences a temporal dissonance. She is that young Susan that Jeffrey fell in love with so many years ago. She has the same shoulder-length brown hair, the same pixie face, the same petite figure. He finds excuses to visit her room and, if she is asleep, he gazes at her for minutes at a time.

Jeffrey is very familiar with the storage area in the basement of the hospital where they keep maintenance supplies and decommissioned equipment. Each night when he finishes his shift he takes a few items home with him, including a can of the paint used throughout the hospital, a pale green Dulux has labelled "Secret Crush."

• • •

Jeffrey has been monitoring Brianna's file in the nursing station to learn exactly when she will be discharged. He takes note that another orderly has been assigned to escort her to a waiting cab when the time comes. Susan was scheduled to work and couldn't be there to take Brianna home. Brianna assures her that she'll be fine going home in a cab. It will be a relief to finally be back in her own bed.

Jeffrey brings a wheelchair to Brianna's room fifteen minutes before the time appointed for her discharge. He also brings some eszopiclone to make her sleep. Once he gets her in the wheelchair, he gives her the pills in a paper cup along with a cup of water. He explains that she is required to take the pills upon discharge.

Jeffrey wheels Brianna down to the main floor and out the front doors. By this time she is sleeping soundly. He takes her past the waiting cab and to his own car in the staff parking area. He moves her gingerly into the backseat of his car.

• • •

As Jeffrey sits at Brianna's bedside gazing at her as she sleeps, he feels as though he has successfully looped back to an earlier time. He feels he is a younger man. He feels he has erased countless regrets and sources of shame.

He feels loved and admired by virtue of the fact that this beautiful young woman is sharing his home.

• • •

On her way home from work Susan stops at a bakery to pick up cinnamon buns, Brianna's favourite. After the days of anxiety and uncertainty in the hospital, she feels a "welcome home" celebration is in order. Perhaps they will watch a movie together as a diversion.

Susan calls out to Brianna as she steps through the front door but there is no response. Thinking Brianna may be napping, she walks quietly to her bedroom but the room is empty and the bed is undisturbed. She then calls out again as she looks in the living room and the den. She checks her phone for messages, but there is nothing.

She tries to think where Brianna might have gone. There is a coffee shop a few blocks away that Brianna is fond of so she decides to walk there to look for her. By the time she gets back home she is feeling panicked. She calls the hospital and they confirm that Brianna was discharged several hours before.

• • •

Brianna has lost sense of how much time has passed. Has she been in the hospital for hours, days, or weeks? When she is awake she feels numb and unable to focus, unsure what she is reliably observing and what she is dreaming in a drug-induced stupor. She recognizes the colour of the walls but everything else in her surroundings is a blur. She wonders why her mother has not been visiting, but perhaps Susan has come while Brianna was asleep.

It occurs to her that she only ever sees the same male nurse who comes to give her more medication. What happened to the other nurses who would help her mark the passage of time with the start of each new shift? An uneasy fear begins to grip Brianna. The fear seems to bring a shade more lucidity. She is able to focus more on her senses. The typical hospital sounds are absent: the beeping of monitors, the anxious calls of distressed patients, the idle conversation of nurses in the corridor. She notes the absence of natural light, knowing that all rooms in the hospital have windows. Even the customary hospital smells seem to have been replaced with a stale, musty odour.

The same male nurse returns to administer more medication just as the last dose is wearing off as though he wants to keep her sedated. Brianna manages to conceal the pills inside her cheek and then remove them when he is not looking. She feels she needs to stay alert and attentive until she understands what is going on.

• • •

Jeffrey checks on Brianna to ensure that she is sleeping comfortably. He then goes upstairs to watch television. Scanning through the channels, he finds that the fictional shows all seem the same while the network news shows are incongruous. The same daily events are reported on each network but with such a contrast of interpretation that it's actually hard to recognize them as the same events. Each channel seems like a different version of reality. In frustration, Jeffrey turns the television off.

He returns to Brianna's bedside. Brianna breathes slowly and shallowly, hoping to properly mimic drug-induced sleep. She steels herself when she senses Jeffrey leaning over her and tries desperately not to flinch when he strokes her hair and softly says, "I love you, Susan."

• • •

Susan contacts the hospital and confirms that the orderly who was assigned to assist with Brianna's discharge found that she had already left. He assumed that Susan had picked her up as he knew Susan was with her every day she was in the hospital. Susan also contacts the cab company and learns that the driver reported a "no show" at the hospital that day.

Susan reports Brianna as a missing person to the police, although she's not convinced they are taking the situation seriously. She then tries to research known sex offenders in the area but is unable to find anything. Lists and databases seem to be available in other jurisdictions, but not where she lives.

Susan returns to the hospital to talk to the doctors, nurses, and other medical staff in the hopes that someone will have a bit of information that might serve as a clue. She goes first to the nursing station that had been responsible for Brianna. There seems to be a tense conversation taking place between a nurse and one of the orderlies. "Jeffrey, consider this a warning. If I catch you taking any drugs or supplies I will have no choice but to report you to Admin. Do you understand?"

Once the nurse is free Susan is able to speak to her. She asks if the nurse recalls anyone else visiting Brianna during her stay in the hospital. Then she has an idea. She asks about the security camera in the lobby. Could those recordings be reviewed for the time when Brianna was discharged? The nurse says a request would have to come from the police.

Susan contacts the police and they agree that examination of the security recordings could be useful. In fact, when the recordings are reviewed, it doesn't take long before they find the footage of Brianna being wheeled out of the hospital. When shown to the head nurse on Brianna's floor she identifies Jeffrey as the person who escorted Brianna from the hospital. Officers are immediately dispatched to his home.

Jeffrey is clearly agitated when the police arrive. Before they have a chance to enter the house to search for Brianna, Jeffrey exclaims apologetically, "Something has gone terribly wrong. It wasn't supposed to work out this way."

GLASS

I push on the clear door of the cabinet that contains the DVD player. After giving the least resistance, the door pops open. I insert a disc and then sit back in an armchair. The music starts with the simple pulsing of a marimba. Almost imperceptibly it is joined by the repetitive stroking of a violin. Over the course of an hour the simple melody line repeats, with other musicians joining in until there are so many instruments it is hard to identify any one individually.

There was a time when I was in constant pursuit of novelty. I loved stepping out into the city knowing there was no way I could predict or control what experiences I might have, who I might meet, how they might alter the course of my life. The city was explosive with possibility and I was ready to welcome whatever random shrapnel I encountered. Since moving north I have craved routine and solitude. I have found solace in the repetitive. I have managed to eliminate chance from my environment.

If I took the events of recent years and transcribed them like a piece of music it would expose the simplicity. There would be no dramatic key changes, no building to a crescendo. It would be more like the scales one practises when learning to play an instrument, over and over, ad nauseum.

After listening to the CD it is time to get outside and do something physical. I strap on my snowshoes for a trek across the frozen bay. The rhythm of the music is embedded in my bones as I set a consistent pace, shifting my weight back and forth, swinging my legs and arms effortlessly. When I reach the mouth of the bay, I pause to scan the horizon. There is a yellow tinge to the sky that suggests a storm is moving in. I don't waste any time returning to the weather station. Despite my efforts to maintain a placid lifestyle, the Arctic weather can impose an element of adventure at any time.

Once I'm safely back indoors, the wind increases alarmingly. Before long the building is straining on its stilts, struggling to resist the wind. I am alternating between checking the instruments and pacing the hallway. The windows are rattling like someone is trying to break in. I go to the kitchen and pour a few ounces of whiskey in a tumbler to calm my nerves. I have to watch my alcohol consumption as I am prone to binge drinking. Also, I have a limited supply of whiskey and it's not something my employer is eager to include in the supply drops.

The whiskey is an effective antidote for my nerves. I go to bed and the rocking of the building actually puts me to sleep.

When I awaken in the morning I am immediately hit with the uneasy feeling that someone else is in the station, which is impossible. I have a figurine of a narwhal on my bureau and I see that it has been moved from its usual spot. Then I hear the CD I was listening to the day before. I go to the living room and I am dumbfounded to see someone sitting in the armchair. I am so stunned I don't say anything. He must be aware of my presence but he doesn't so much as glance in my direction.

I decide to avoid the living room for the remainder of the day as though the intruder might disappear if I refuse to acknowledge him. I perform my required duties in the lab and in the office, make a sandwich for dinner, and then go to bed early.

My night is animated with bizarre dreams. One dream in particular sticks with me. A behemoth rises from the bay and is, in fact, composed entirely of ice. He chases me out onto the land, where I struggle to find traction. When he is finally about to lay his hands on me, I awaken in a cold sweat. I get out of bed feeling emotionally fragile. I almost forget about my mysterious guest in the living room. Just before having a shower, I go to check. My heart sinks to find him still sitting in the armchair, just as I'd last seen him. I turn away and am terrified to see a second intruder, this time in the kitchen, at the sink, with his back to me. Again, I retreat to my work areas, although it is worse than the day before since I now need to avoid the kitchen as well as the living room. I go the entire day without eating.

After another restless night I awaken to the realization that someone is in the bedroom with me. I feel this even before I open my eyes and see three indistinct figures in the early morning light. I start out of bed and find that people are milling about in the corridor. I seek refuge in the shower but I find two people, fully clothed, occupying the shower. None of these people seems to register my presence or, for that matter, each other.

I don't see any choice but to leave. I strap on my snowshoes and walk to the mouth of the bay. Then I keep going.

FISH

Place filets with marinade on a cast iron pan or baking dish and bake for thirty-five to forty minutes or until filets are cooked through. Make sure to flip the filets a few times so that the meat will be juicy and tender without getting dry on top. Finally, broil on high for five minutes or until the filets have a beautiful roasted colour. Garnish with chopped parsley. Serve with rice or mashed potato and make sure to pour the sauce over the filets when serving.

Albert spent a day cleaning and disinfecting the upstairs bedroom and the kitchen, as well as doing the laundry. Then he sat down to a backlog of email. He responded thoughtfully and meticulously to all the messages that warranted response. He had missed deadlines on a few items but nothing that would result in negative repercussions.

The next day was Sunday, so Albert put on a dress shirt, pants fresh from the dry cleaners, and newly polished shoes and went to mass. He walked down the sunny side of Dufferin until he arrived at St. Peter's. He crossed the street and took his usual pew. As always, his eyes were drawn to the crucifix suspended over the transept. While Albert was normally calmed by the familiar ritual of mass, on this occasion he became restless during the sacrament of communion. He started to feel nauseous at the thought of accepting a wafer from the priest. After growing increasingly agitated, he abruptly got to his feet and departed, something he had never done before.

To calm his nerves, Albert decided to take a walk along the river to an area they called the flood plains. He never understood why it was referred to that way since he'd never known the river to overflow its banks. He always knew it as an area he could rely on to be sparsely populated by humans but where the bird population was plentiful. He was particularly pleased when he encountered a bobolink nesting in the dead grasses.

As he was walking a path leading out of the flood plains he was stopped by two police officers. They looked at him suspiciously and asked where he had been, where he was headed. They asked what he did for a living. They asked if he had seen anything unusual during his walk. Albert explained that he had been to mass and was then indulging in a walk in nature before heading home. He explained that he was a computer technician working for one of the big office supply chains. And, no, he didn't recall noticing anything unusual.

"A young girl has gone missing in this area. We'd ask you to be alert and notify us immediately if you see anything out of the ordinary."

Albert assured them he would do that.

This interaction with the police caused Albert's anxiety level to soar once again. As he walked home, his focus was almost entirely at his feet. The rhythm of his steps flashed in sync with his heartbeat. His jaw was clenched and sweat began bleeding down his face and back. His once gleaming dress shoes were now hardly recognizable as black beneath the dirt and dust from his hike.

Albert realized that it was time to dispose of the packages in his freezer and the articles of clothing. He didn't want to decide on the best place for disposal because, he reasoned, if he could identify a location using linear logic then someone else could come up with the same location using the same logic. Instead, he decided to use a system of chance in order to randomize the choice of a site. Employing a combination of Google Maps and numerology, he pinpointed a spot ninety-five kilometres away. He could see on Google Maps that it was an area of farmland with a sizeable forest just off a country road.

Albert loaded the frozen packages, clothing, and a spade in the trunk of his car and drove to the spot outside a hamlet called Everett. He parked the car behind an abandoned barn and walked from there into the bush. He found a spot by a stream where there was a clearing big enough for his digging. By the time he was done, the packages were beginning to thaw and the smell made bile rise in his throat. He was glad he'd made the hole as deep as he had. Once he moved the earth back it seemed unlikely that any animals would dig anything up.

The next day Albert saw "missing girl" posters starting to appear around the neighbourhood. He was standing outside a pharmacy studying one.

The girl's name was Gracie. The photo they used showed her made up for a special event, perhaps her First Communion. She was last seen playing in a park with several other children. The poster described what she was wearing and also mentioned that she had her favourite doll with her.

"What a lovely girl. We can only pray that she will be found safe and unharmed."

Albert was startled and turned to look at the woman who had appeared beside him in front of the poster. He walked away without responding.

He stopped at a cafe and ordered an Earl Grey tea, which he sipped slowly until it was cold. A woman in the cafe was breastfeeding her child. Albert caught himself staring at her and looked away before she noticed. He listened to a number of conversations between other customers in the cafe. For some reason most of them seemed to be about health issues and the quality of health care that had been provided.

Albert's thoughts turned to familiar patterns of self-doubt and guilt. He thought of times he had failed to live up to people's expectations. From his youth to more recent years, from small incidents through major transgressions. There seemed to be no end of regrets that plagued him and kept him awake at night. He read an article once about the global problem of food wastage and now, whenever something in his fridge expired and he had to dispose of it, he added it to his burden of guilt.

By the time he got back home, Albert was experiencing heartburn. He went to the bureau in his bedroom where he kept medication and took an antacid pill. He decided to lie down for a while until he felt better but first he opened the cedar chest at the foot of his bed and took out Gracie's doll. He stretched out on his bed, embracing her.

CHARTREUSE

When Kellie first arrived at the home, I recognized her right away. She had been a very attractive young woman and the years had not stolen her beauty. Forty years ago I fell in love with her while also finding her somewhat intimidating. Part of that was her height. Part of it was her intensity. She seemed to be smouldering all the time. There was nothing light or frivolous about her. She rarely smiled, but often laughed. She was like a diamond, all sharp edges and refracted light.

On her first day at the home I watched her walk tentatively through the lounge. I turned to Jackie and commented on the new arrival. I could see in Jackie's eyes that she didn't approve of Kellie or of my interest in Kellie. Jackie didn't trust anyone new until they had been there long enough to prove themselves. "Her name is Kellie. I believe the man who brought her here was her son." After relaying this information to me, Jackie seemed to study me, waiting for a reaction. I was determined not to betray my interest but I also knew that I wasn't good at masking my feelings.

The first time we spoke at the home was when Kellie stopped me in the hall and asked me where the library was. I offered to walk her there as it was just a few steps away. Apologetically, she said, "Someone showed me where it is but I seem to be disoriented. Thanks so much."

Before she entered the small room we called the library, I ventured to ask, "You don't remember me, do you?"

"I'm sorry. Please don't take offense. My memory has been unreliable and getting worse by the day. It's nothing personal, I assure you."

"Don't worry. It was almost forty years ago. Another lifetime, really. How is your son, Billy?"

Kellie seemed taken aback but then seemed to let down her guard just a bit. "You know Billy? He's doing well. He's head of research and development with a chemical firm. Married, two kids. A son named Tim and a daughter named . . . oh damn! What is her name?"

"Not a problem. Don't worry."

It is appropriate that my first attempt to reconnect with Kellie was focused on Billy because Billy was the reason we got together. Kellie had been seeing a man named Doug before we met but she didn't view him as a good father figure. She was drawn to me because she felt I would fill that role. I am soft-spoken, patient, steady. Those are not qualities for a passionate lover, but they may be desirable in a father.

A few days later I passed Kellie when she was struggling to carry several books from the library. I asked her if she needed a hand. "Actually, there's one other book I signed out but I couldn't quite manage it. If you don't mind grabbing that, it would be a big help." I found the book on the reading table and followed Kellie to her room. She thanked me and then suggested we meet in the lounge for a drink sometime.

I saw her around the home off and on for the next week or so but never really had an excuse to engage her in conversation. Then, seemingly out of the blue, at the end of the afternoon on a Thursday, she approached me in the lobby and asked, "So, how about today? Would you be up for a drink?"

We found a quiet corner in the lounge. As we chatted I found it was still quite easy to spend time with her. I noticed a bottle of Chartreuse behind the bar. I mentioned this to Kellie and she said she'd never tried Chartreuse. Although we drank Chartreuse often those many years ago, I simply said, "Well, there's no time like the present."

When our drinks arrived we toasted each other and then Kellie, not seeming at all self-conscious about her memory issues, asked me to fill in the history that she was unable to recall. "So, remind me how we used to know each other. I'm sure it will come back to me as we talk."

• • •

"Well, we were actually a couple for a period of time.

"I was making a living as a graphic artist but I had always enjoyed working with kids so I volunteered to run a community program teaching cartoon drawing on Saturday mornings. Billy was one of the kids who came to my classes and we really hit it off. I remember one time when I was drawing something and the kids were gathered around me. Billy was playing with the hairs on my arm and then he paused, looked up at me, and said, 'You know, you've got enough hair there you could patch your forehead.'

"When Billy's birthday came around he really wanted me to come to his party. I was more than happy to accept the invitation. I spent the afternoon with you and Billy and three of his friends from the neighbourhood. That's when you and I became acquainted. I stayed for dinner that day and, before long, I was spending more time at your place than at my own. You were a single mother so we never really had the opportunity for typical dating. Most evenings I'd help you make dinner and stay the night. On weekends we'd take Billy on day trips in the area.

"That went on for a number of months and then your ex, Doug, came back into your life. You told me that you'd never stopped being in love with him and you wanted to give it another go. It broke my heart but I did my best to make a graceful withdrawal. That was the last I saw of you until you moved in here.

"I have very fond memories of those days with you and Billy. I remember one evening in particular when I got to read Billy his bedtime story. At that time he was a bit obsessed with a series of horror stories for children called *Goosebumps*. I read to him while you sat nearby, listening and watching.

"The story we read that night featured a boy and girl who decided to explore a deserted home. It was evident that the house had been gutted by fire. Many charred objects from the family who had lived there lay scattered about. Most surprising was a child's taffeta dress hanging in a closet looking not at all damaged by fire or time. The author described its colour as chartreuse. Billy asked me what colour that was. The girl in the story put the dress on over what she was wearing. That's when things took a turn for the supernatural. The boy disappeared and the girl began exploring the house alone and found that, unlike moments before, it was fully furnished and in pristine condition. It seems the dress had transported her back in time.

"She picked up an oil lamp from an end table and began exploring one room after another. She found that one of the bedrooms was locked but she'd seen an old skeleton key near the fireplace so she retraced her steps to get the key. Sure enough, it did open the door. In that bedroom she was shocked to see a life-size portrait of a girl who looked just like her. What's more, she was wearing the same taffeta dress. The girl placed the lamp in front of the painting so that she could spend some time studying it. She noted that the girl in the painting was holding a Japanese fan. But while gazing at the painting she accidentally knocked over the lamp. The oil spilled and caught fire. The girl tried to leave the room but the door had somehow locked behind her. In no time the room was engulfed in flames. Choking and sweating, the girl was in a state of panic. On a desperate hunch she removed the taffeta dress. Immediately, as the dress cleared her head, she felt a rush of cool, fresh air. Her eyes gradually cleared and she found herself back in the charred remains of the old house. She walked back to the living room and found the young boy occupied in his own explorations. He had hardly noticed that she had been absent. Then he looked down at her hand.

"'What have you found there?'"

"She was holding an ancient Japanese fan."

• • •

Kellie looked at me for a full minute as though she were trying to decide how to react. Finally she said, "Well, you're a good storyteller. We'll have to do this again sometime."

I watched her get up and walk toward her room. Then I looked at the remnants of the Chartreuse in her glass.

KENNEL

Last week I passed by my friend Francine's place and realized I was overdue to check in on her. She had suffered a heart attack in the spring and while her recovery was going well there was still cause for vigilance. So I dropped in on her on this day. She put on a pot of tea and reassured me that she was doing well.

She had adopted a new puppy since the last time I had been there. The puppy was nervous around me at first, even growling tentatively from behind Francine's leg. But eventually he realized I was not a threat and started sniffing me. I stayed very still for a while until I felt he trusted me and then I slowly began to stroke his little head. By the time my visit was over he was snuggling in my lap. I have to say that the rapid process of winning a little creature's trust endeared him to me.

I promised to check in on Francine again the following week.

I couldn't get her puppy off my mind and so I decided to visit the humane society to see about adopting one of my own. It's funny because I'd never really considered having a dog before. I always thought it would tie me down too much. We did have a dog when I was a child but as I aged I thought I'd never again share my home with a pet of any sort.

Once I met Corey I knew adoption was beyond doubt. I sensed a sympathetic soul when I looked into his eyes. He seemed appreciative of attention without being needy or hyper. I immediately started the process of making him my own.

• • •

It always saddens me to see street dogs. Sometimes they are lying indolently in the sun, ignoring the people stepping around them. Sometimes they are rooting around in the alleys, looking for scraps of food. Sometimes they are on the move in packs of three or four, in which case I cross to the other side of the street to ensure they don't view me as a threat.

• • •

I awoke last night with a racing heart after a bad dream. I was on a leisurely walk on a trail, enjoying the wildflowers and the warm breeze. The trail led me to a higher altitude where I could take in the view of rolling hills. The farther I walked the narrower the trail became. Soon I had a wall of stone on my right and a sheer drop on my left. The trail itself turned from firm soil to loose rock. Each step dislodged pebbles that cascaded into the abyss. When I rounded a bend I saw that my passage was blocked by a dog with bared teeth, frothing at the mouth. I tried to turn back but by that point the trail was so diminished that I lost my footing. I managed to grab some secure rocks before I slipped over the edge. As I hung by my fingers, the dog started snapping at my hands. I felt his saliva dropping onto my face. Just as my fingers slipped from their rocky purchase, I awoke in a panic.

I lay in bed listening to the distant sound of street dogs barking to each other in the moonlight.

• • •

Until recently Corey had been the most affectionate of housemates. Whenever I came home he would jump and wriggle as though he couldn't contain his joy. He would then follow me around the house, try to crawl onto my lap whenever I sat down, and basically look at me adoringly throughout the evening. As of late I notice he seems to be growing out of that behaviour. Increasingly he seems indifferent to my presence. He occasionally seems to actively avoid me by going to the basement when I am upstairs. Being a new dog owner I have to assume this is a normal part of maturation.

• • •

I heard on the news today that a jogger was attacked and killed by dogs on the Riverside Trail. Apparently it was the fifth attack in the city this month, but the first time someone was killed. The police are using surveillance footage to try to identify the dogs involved, but, given the number of street dogs in the city, it seems unlikely that they could make that determination. They can't indiscriminately kill all the dogs in the city.

• • •

When I took Corey for his morning walk today we encountered a pack of six dogs near the park. They approached us in a menacing manner with hackles raised and lips curled, gradually fanning out and encircling us. My fear increased as they closed in, growling and snarling. I was aware that other dogs were gathering on the block as though monitoring the situation before potentially joining an attack.

Corey, feeling threatened but also sensing my distress, finally lunged at the apparent alpha male in the pack. This proved enough to disperse the group at least momentarily. I took advantage of the stand-off by leading Corey quickly back to the house. An assortment of dogs followed us, but kept their distance.

• • •

Politicians are debating an appropriate strategy to deal with the street dogs problem. One proposal is the sterilization of all street dogs. Apart from being a logistical nightmare, it would take years to see an actual decrease in the number of dogs. Another idea is to create a compound where street dogs could be relocated. The compound would need to be nearly as large as the city itself and, once created, would be impossible to manage. In many ways the most practical and immediate solution would be mass extermination of all street dogs.

• • •

Things were different when I was young. As a ten-year-old boy I would be off with my friends seeking adventure for much of the day on the weekend and for several hours after school during the week. We would pack a lunch and go for a day-long hike along the railway tracks.

One day I was exploring with my friend Murray. We loved to find abandoned buildings or we'd go to the village dump, where there were piles of rusted-out cars. Even at that age we sensed that these forgotten places and objects carried the remnants of lives lived and lives lost. On this day we clambered over dented fenders and busted headlights in the dump looking for treasures but all we found was a wasp nest in an old Dodge Dart.

On the walk home dusk was settling in and I was a little anxious that I would be late for dinner. My mom didn't worry about me when I was away from the house but she did want me at the table in time for dinner. As we walked we began to hear a strange bellowing. It sounded like a dog but not a normal dog's sound. Murray suddenly grabbed my arm and said, "That's a dog with rabies! We need to get home before he catches up with us." We ran to our separate homes. My heart was pounding with fear. Even at the time, I was unsure whether Murray was as terrified as I was or simply egging me on.

• • •

The government has issued an advisory telling everyone to remain in their homes due to the increasing incidence of dog attacks. There is some inconsistency in the messaging. In some cases the wording is along the lines of "remain in your home unless going out is absolutely necessary." In other cases you hear "if you go out for exercise or fresh air, remain close to your home so that you can return to safety at the first sign of trouble."

I have been strategic about my grocery shopping so as to minimize both the number of times I go shopping and the amount of time I spend outside when I do go out. This means favouring things that I can buy in bulk that will keep for a longer period of time. The strategy has to be flexible, however, because many people have begun hoarding and so things I intend to buy are not necessarily available.

I am an introvert by nature, so I really don't mind being alone all day, but I find that, over time, I miss being around people, interacting with people, even making physical contact with people. Having Corey in the house helps. I talk to him, play with him, cuddle with him when he lets me but I still long to be in the presence of other humans.

• • •

I have been feeling increasingly uneasy around Corey. He has been watching my every move, but keeping his distance. When I have tried to approach him, he's emitted a barely audible growl. This morning when I emerged from the bedroom, he immediately began growling in a more threatening manner. I approached him and, in a soothing tone, said, "Corey, boy. What's the matter?" He lunged at me and snapped his teeth so close to my face that I could smell his breath. I managed to retreat into the bedroom and close the door.

After an hour or so I decided to test the situation, but when I opened the door a crack I saw that he was stationed right in front of it. He lunged again and began barking ferociously. When I closed the door, he scratched at it with his claws for a good thirty minutes before relenting.

Since then I have not dared to venture out of the bedroom. I can't make sense of the situation.

• • •

I have been sequestered in my bedroom for thirty-six hours. I have been monitoring developments outside by listening to my bedside radio, but I haven't been able to access my phone or computer as they are in the living room.

The city is in crisis mode. No one is permitted outdoors without armed escorts. To date, an estimated 4,500 people have been killed by the growing numbers of street dogs. Efforts are being made to evacuate people by trains and airplanes, although it is uncertain where it is safe for people to go. Automobile travel is forbidden as there is no safe way to obtain fuel. The military has secured small areas of the city using armoured vehicles and forces in full riot gear. As I understand it, one of these safe zones is about five kilometres from my home.

• • •

As I've had no food or water in two days and as the situation outside seems to grow worse the longer I wait, I've decided to leave and try to make my way to the safe zone. Based solely on my own monitoring of dog noises I've determined that late morning is the optimal time to venture out. The dogs are very active through the night into the dawn hours. I sense they spend the heat of midday dozing in shaded areas. By leaving around 10:00 a.m., I should have several hours to make the hike.

I open the bedroom window and crawl outside. The street seems quiet and deserted, as I hoped it would be. As I am making my way cautiously down the street I feel a pang of guilt as I realize that Corey is locked in the house with no food or water.

GENERATION

Do you know what a kidnapper is? A kidnapper is someone who takes a child to be his own. I can barely remember my real family now.

My kidnapper wore green T-shirts. You could see the bulge of his belly in his T-shirts. For some reason, I didn't notice the bulge as much when he was naked. He was naked when he came to see me in the basement at night after he'd been drinking.

It was my job to wash his T-shirts in the laundry tub. Sometimes, my blood was on his T-shirts, and then I had to scrub them very hard.

It was also my job to make soft-boiled eggs for his lunch. I boiled the eggs for six-and-a-half minutes. Then I bounced the eggs on the counter to crack their shells. Then I carefully peeled off the shells. I couldn't leave any bits of shell on the egg or he would get angry.

A man came to the house one day while I was upstairs in the kitchen making eggs. That had never happened before. My kidnapper seemed very nervous, like I might call out to the visitor, or make a sudden dash for the open door. But I had no inclination to do either of those things. I would have liked to see the man, though. It had been a long time since I'd seen any face but my kidnapper's.

After this visit from the unknown man, my kidnapper locked me in the basement for a long time. I was getting hungry by the time he finally let me come up. Perhaps he was frightened by the man's visit and wanted to be sure no one else would show up.

And then people did come to the house. I was in the basement that time and could only hear muffled conversation. I could tell there was at least one woman and one man talking to my kidnapper but no matter how hard I tried I couldn't make out what they were saying. Eventually I heard their footsteps move to the basement door. Then I heard the familiar sound of the key turning in the lock.

"Another reason I keep this door locked is because the stairs are unsafe. I don't want any visitors getting curious and then hurting themselves."

I could hear their conversation clearly when the door was open.

"Are you going to want to look around in the basement? If so, I'd need to get a flashlight. There are no working lights down there."

That was a lie. There was a bare bulb that could be turned on and off with a string.

The woman responded, "No, not at this time. I think we've seen enough for now. We'll be in touch."

At first I thought they might have come to the house looking for me. But if that were true, why would they not look down in the basement? It made no sense. On the one hand I was disappointed, but I was also relieved. I decided to leave a clue for the next time visitors came to the house.

"Be careful," I told myself as I brought my shoes up from the basement. If he guessed what I was up to, he'd give me a beating. I had no use for the shoes since I was never allowed to leave the house. Besides, they no longer fit me as I'd grown since he first brought me there. But I decided to put them in the vestibule, hoping he wouldn't notice. But maybe the visitors would see the shoes and wonder why a little girl's shoes would be in this house.

Believe it or not, he never did take note of my shoes. The house was full of random junk, so it was not like he would be inclined to notice things being out of place. Besides, he was not the most observant person. He could be ultra-fussy about some things and then oblivious to other things. He was particularly upset if he found blood stains on my clothes. Sometimes I scrubbed until the fabric ripped. Fortunately, my kidnapper occasionally brought new clothes for me from Walmart. He had terrible taste in clothes. Usually there was some sort of cartoon character on them that I didn't even recognize. I guess if I could have watched TV I would have known them.

"Centro" was printed on the last T-shirt he bought for me. I thought it was an Italian word but I didn't know what it meant. I believe he bought the cheapest things he could find. Maybe they were second-hand.

I was a child when he brought me here. What am I now? I don't feel like a child anymore but I'm not a woman. Childhood was laughter. Childhood was toys and games. Childhood was playing on the lawn with my brother until my mom called us in for dinner. Childhood was summer vacations at the beach. That life in my kidnapper's basement was not childhood.

The visitors eventually returned. As before, I heard footsteps and talking, but wasn't able to discern what was being said. Then the door to the basement opened and I heard the same woman's voice say, "My colleagues will wait up here while you show me around the basement." Then I listened to their footsteps descending the stairs. I have no idea what they were expecting to find in the basement.

VOLLEY

"OK, we're going to finish by doing some work on your volleying. Come up to the net. I'm going to have you moving around a lot, so stay on your toes."

Ken took balls out of the basket and fed them to Scotty one after another, sometimes forcing a backhand, sometimes a forehand, sometimes making him move laterally, occasionally hitting a lob that would make him shuffle back and hit an overhead smash.

A woman from the next court caused them to pause as she needed to leave a bit early. Ken glanced at her legs, which stretched from her tennis shoes to her pleated skirt as she passed through their court. He forced himself to look away as he didn't need to develop a reputation for lechery.

He emptied the basket of tennis balls and then announced the end of Scotty's lesson.

"I'm assuming you want to develop your game to the point that you can play competitively at the club. If that's the case, then at our next lesson we need to work more on your serve. Remind your dad to e-transfer fifty dollars for today's lesson."

Ken refilled the basket of balls and then took it to the corner where they were kept. He locked the lid on the basket to ensure the balls wouldn't disappear before the next lesson he had to deliver. He watched a group of retired men file onto the courts for the weekly house league. Then he went out to the parking lot and waved to Scotty's dad.

• • •

Scotty's dad was waiting for Scotty in the car in front of the club. As Scotty got in the car his dad asked, "How was your lesson?"

"It's always good."

"Did Ken say anything about how much progress you're making?"

"He says I'll be ready for competition soon. I think I'm his favourite student. Just like I'm your favourite son."

Scotty's dad laughed.

When Scotty got home he went up to his room to text his girlfriend, Lisa. The last time they got together they went further than they'd ever gone before. Now Scotty could hardly wait to see her again. They had a date to see a movie on Thursday.

• • •

On Thursday Ken decided it was time to clean up around the shed in his backyard. It was an area where things got dumped as sort of a way station before their eventual disposal. As he neared the shed, he became aware of an unpleasant odour. It brought back memories of his grandfather's basement, which was dark and musty, filled with spiders, and with a crawl space that had a dirt floor. That basement was repugnant but it was the perfect place for a young boy to explore. He hadn't thought of his grandfather's basement in thirty years.

Behind an old plastic bucket he found the source of the stench. A mouse had been beheaded and was now churning with maggots. Repulsed, Ken shovelled the carcass into the bucket, put the bucket in a garbage bag, and dropped it in his bin at the side of the house. Feeling sullied by the experience, he looked accusingly at the neighbour's property to the north. On too many occasions, he had spied their cat prowling in his yard, treading tentatively.

• • •

Treading tentatively, Scotty asked Lisa if she had ever kissed a boy before him. She said she'd had a boyfriend the previous summer but they'd broken up after two months.

"Who was he? Do I know him?"

Lisa replied, "Oh, you know him. I'm not going to tell you who it was, but I'll give you clues and see if you can figure it out." Scotty agreed to the challenge.

"Remember last year's city track and field meet? How many events did you enter?"

"My best event was the 400-metre race. I won my preliminary race and then came third in the finals. I didn't do as well in the 100-metre dash. And I also competed in the long jump and the high jump. So, four events, I guess. Next year I want to try the decathlon."

"Well," Lisa said with a hint of mischief in her voice, "my old boyfriend beat you in one of those events."

Scotty found himself getting angry and flustered. He not only came second in kissing Lisa but also lost in some athletic competition, but he didn't even know who this other boy was. "OK, I don't really feel like guessing right now. I'll give it some thought."

. . .

Some thought fracking would be a boost to the economy while most people were more concerned about the damage to the local groundwater. City council was hosting an all-candidates' debate for the upcoming municipal elections and Ken knew it would provide a good opportunity to find out where the candidates stood on this issue.

The weather had been wet and unseasonably cold, which had kept him hunkered down at home for the previous two days. He enjoyed the walk to city hall on this milder autumn evening. Once he arrived at city hall, Ken walked down the corridor to the main auditorium where the debate was taking place. He picked a seat away from the most congested area. As he was settling in a woman behind him said, "Ken . . . Ken Greenham, is that you?"

He recognized the woman as a girl he knew in high school. In fact, he had had a crush on her for years. "Melanie, my goodness. I haven't seen you in decades. You look great."

As they traded biographical details, he learned that she had a son, aged fourteen. It occurred to him that his tennis student Scotty was the same age as the boy.

. . .

The boy who had kissed Lisa didn't prove to be much of a mystery to Scotty. As soon as he thought back to the track meet, it was obvious to him that the other boy was Tommy Klein. Tommy was a good-looking, athletic boy who was popular with both the boys and the girls at school. Scotty always felt inadequate compared to Tommy but not because Tommy acted superior.

Scotty wrote a note on a scrap of paper and taped it to Tommy's locker. It read, "Meet me at the main entrance of the school at 4:00 p.m."

At the end of the school day, Scotty went to the front doors of the school. Tommy was already there with a couple of friends. Scotty swallowed his fear and tried his best to project confidence and nonchalance. When he got close, Tommy gave him a genuinely warm smile. "Hey, Scotty. I haven't seen you in a while. You have something you want to talk about?"

"Hey, Tommy. Ya, I want to ask you a favour. Last year at the track and field meet you beat me at the 400-metre race. I think I'm faster now. Would you be willing to race me again? Just an unofficial one-on-one challenge race. What do you say?"

Tommy laughed and said, "Sure, Scotty. That sounds like fun. How about Saturday morning?"

• • •

"Saturday morning for coffee then." Ken and Melanie agreed to meet and get caught up with each other. Ken felt a little uneasy about the date but he found it amusing to think what a nervous wreck he would have been had this opportunity come up in their high school years.

As he was leaving city hall, he witnessed a protester being arrested. Based on the sign left behind it would seem that the target of his protest was one of the pro-fracking candidates. The protester had sprayed blood on the stone walls of city hall.

Ken decided to walk home and go to bed early with the novel he was currently reading on his iPad.

• • •

His iPad pinged, alerting Scotty to a message. It was Lisa saying she had to cancel their movie date because her dad had had a stroke. He had been at the pool for his weekly swim when it happened. Lisa and her mom were at the hospital waiting to hear the prognosis.

Scotty took his racket to the tennis courts at school and worked on his serve. He was pleased with the velocity of the serve but felt he needed to improve on his accuracy. He struggled a bit with his toss because it required looking straight into the sun.

• • •

The sun was strong so Ken and Melanie found a bench under a tree where they took their coffee. Melanie told Ken about meeting her husband in university. Her parents still lived in the house in the suburbs where she grew up. Ken explained that he had never married. He got a tennis scholarship and then played professionally for over a decade. The travel and dedication to training meant there really wasn't much opportunity to develop relationships.

Eventually, the conversation came around to the debate at city hall. It turned out Melanie was quite passionate about the fracking issue and that's what had motivated her to attend. As she talked about the long-term damage to the ecosystem Ken's attention was drawn to an artist who was setting up under a nearby tree. He had an easel, a stool, a paintbox, and a jar.

• • •

A jar in Scotty's closet contained a collection of his most precious items. From that jar he removed his lucky coin, which he'd found one summer. It had been buried in the sand at the beach and was minted in the year of his birth. He placed the coin in the pocket of his gym shorts before heading to the track at his school.

Tommy was already there waiting for him with the same two friends who had been there when Scotty had issued the challenge. They didn't waste any time taking their positions on the track. One of the friends counted down from three and they took off. Scotty got a jump on Tommy with a good start and built his lead over the first 200 metres. But then his breathing became more laboured, his stride less fluid. He realized he hadn't paced himself as well as he should have. By the time they made a full lap around the track, Tommy was several strides ahead of him.

They both sat on the grass to catch their breath. Tommy congratulated him on a strong effort. "I guess I just have your number. But we'll try again sometime. I'm sure you'll beat me eventually."

One of Tommy's friends asked Scotty, "Are you going with Lisa? Someone told me you were her new boyfriend."

Scotty replied, "Well, kind of, I guess."

"Well, you should buy some condoms. Small condoms."

Tommy interjected, "What a stupid thing to say! Don't mind him, Scotty. He can be a jerk sometimes."

Scotty served to Ken's backhand. Ken's return was deep, just inside the baseline. Scotty hit an effortless forehand. Ken responded with a drop shot that brought Scotty to the net. He chipped a backhand and then waited to volley the next shot. Ken sent a lob high over Scotty's head, causing him to shuffle back, staring straight up at the ball, impatient for its descent.

DAMILOLA

Every Thursday evening Damilola Akpata would go to La Whiskey for a nightcap, to unwind near the end of the work week and begin the transition to the weekend. He would nurse a single Legend Extra Stout while watching the other patrons and listening to the radio behind the bar. He was generally left in peace and he cherished this scheduled hour of self-indulgence.

On this night he was somewhat disappointed to see a familiar face in the bar. He felt obliged to make conversation. "Ajibola, how are you, my friend?"

While Damilola may have been discomfited by the obligation to be social, Ajibola was clearly flustered. "Ah, Damilola! Please, have a seat. What a surprise. I've never been here before and didn't expect to see anyone I know."

"But are you sure I'm not disturbing you?"

"It's OK. I have something I need to do and I just came in here for a shot of scotch to steel my nerves." Ajibola looked nervously down at his backpack on the floor and nudged it a bit closer to his chair.

Just then the radio announced the opening of the twentieth Oil and Gas Conference. The broadcaster asserted that it was an event to be celebrated as there would be many international delegates forming strategic partnerships and boosting the economy. Having said that, there were concerns about violent protests focused on the inequitable distribution of wealth from the booming industry.

It was clear to Damilola that the report on the radio had captured all of Ajibola's attention. All he had to do was raise his eyebrows at Ajibola to get him to open up. "Our concerns must be heard and sometimes that requires extreme measures. The opening reception is taking place now at the Eko Hotel. I need to get there now."

"Ajibola, what are you intending to do?"

"You can read about it in the papers tomorrow, my friend."

"Don't be foolhardy!"

"I must go."

Ajibola grabbed his backpack and left abruptly. Damilola sat in confusion for a moment, then raced after him, grabbing a diner's knife from a nearby table. He caught up with Ajibola before he reached the Eko. He threw him up against a wall and pressed the knife along his cheek.

"I don't want anyone to get hurt but I will kill you if that's what it takes to keep innocent people safe at the hotel. This is a foolish plan."

Ajibola dropped the backpack. "I know you are right. I'm not even sure I was going to follow through with it. I've just been so angry and frustrated."

"What we're going to do is throw your backpack into the Kuramo Waters. Then we're going back to La Whiskey for another drink. We need to talk."

After disposing of the backpack, they started for the bar but only got as far as Olosa Street when they saw a major protest taking place on Adetokunbo Ademola. Protesters had blocked the intersection and counter-protesters were confronting them. Ajibola turned to Damilola and said, "I'm sorry, my friend. We'll have to have that drink another time. I need to lend my support. Thank you. You saved my life today."

Damilola walked to the SunCity Hotel, where he had been living for the last year. After he arrived he took his *kontigi* onto the balcony and played for half an hour. Because he was recognized for his musical talent, he had been asked to perform at a community fundraiser. He was in the habit of practising every evening before bed time.

In the morning, Damilola took the long ride by danfo to the shoe factory where he worked as a supply-chain manager. He had a small radio on his desk and was listening to the daily news when he heard a bulletin that shocked him.

"Protests outside the Oil and Gas Conference turned violent last night. There were a number of minor injuries and over twenty people were arrested. The police are uncertain whether a death in the area was related to the protests. The victim has been identified as Ajibola Adedotun. He was discovered near Olosa Street, where he died of knife wounds. Investigators are asking anyone who witnessed anything that might be pertinent to contact the police immediately."

Damilola thought he had saved Ajibola from losing his life in a reckless suicide attack, but his passionate beliefs had led to his demise regardless. He disregarded the request to contact the police as he didn't trust them. They were known to be particularly harsh in their treatment of protesters, so it wouldn't serve him well to be allied with Ajibola. Besides, Ajibola wanted to give his life for his cause and he accomplished that. There was nothing more that could be done for him.

His decision not to notify the police became moot as two officers found Damilola at his desk before the end of the work day. He was ordered to accompany them to the police station, where he was led into an airless cube of a room.

"We have a witness who saw you with Ajibola Adedotun at the La Whiskey bar the night he was murdered. What's more, you were seen grabbing a knife and following him into the street. Can you tell us what happened when you left the bar?"

Damilola related the events in the most honest and straightforward manner.

"Would you have considered this Ajibola to be a friend of yours?"

"Yes, not a close friend, but we had socialized together. We know many of the same people."

"And so you're asking us to believe that you would have gladly taken the life of your friend to save the lives of people you had never met?"

"It is the nature of a suicide bomber that his life would have been lost regardless."

"And it is a coincidence that, while you pursued him, prepared to take his life, he was discovered murdered by multiple stab wounds shortly thereafter? It seems you had intent and the results speak for themselves, wouldn't you say?"

"I know it looks bad, but that's not what happened. I didn't kill Ajibola."

The interrogators quite abruptly grabbed Damilola by the arms, and led him out of the room and down a long corridor to a cell. A jailor pushed him into the cell and gave him a sharp blow with a cane before locking the door. They left him there without any explanation of how the interrogation might be resumed.

About an hour passed before another jailor arrived and opened the cell door. "You're being released."

Damilola was skeptical. "How can that be? The investigators believe I am a murderer."

"Maybe they do, maybe they don't. It doesn't really matter. If you're innocent, you're harmless; if you're guilty, you're useful. Have a good weekend, my friend."

Damilola started making his way to the SunCity Hotel, but then decided to stop in first at La Whiskey. He felt like a Legend Extra Stout, but he also wanted to compensate them for the missing knife. He hoped to continue patronizing his favourite watering hole and thought it might be prudent to supplant the last image of him chasing after another customer with a stolen knife.

QUARRY

After the initial shock subsided, the hardest thing to endure has been the tedium. There is nothing to do. With no light source we can't even see each other or our surroundings. Now and then someone sings a song and a few others might join in half-heartedly. Alternately someone will cry and then it seems like all nine of us are crying.

I was barely aware of the sound of the air ventilator until now, when it suddenly stopped. The battery on the generator must have expired. The silence is startling at first. Laura, who is next to me, grabs my arm. "We're going to run out of oxygen, aren't we?" Her fear is causing her to breathe rapidly, which can't be good for our air supply.

• • •

I'm riding the packed, rush-hour subway home. I'm squeezed so tight against Reynolds that I can hear the music playing on his headphones. It's some sort of Latin pop dance music. His belly is pressing against my arm. I smell his sweat and his breath. His sister, Rebecca, is next to him. She has a giant Slurpee from the 7-Eleven. The sound of her slurping is continuous, making me wonder if she ever exhales.

Parker has her back to me. She hasn't been speaking to me lately. I'm not sure why, but I suspect it is because she feels I humiliated her in front of her peers. She takes a lot of pride in her education and experience and, when I pointed out she was violating public health guidelines, she took that as a deliberate attack on her status. At least, that's my best guess as to the cause of her hostility.

From the first time I saw Sandy, her beauty has left me breathless. She is wearing a royal blue top that sets off her dark hair and fair complexion. She is grasping the subway pole beside me in a way that leaves her bare forearm inches from my face. I fight the urge to lean forward and press my lips against her skin.

"Stop pushing!" Jennifer snaps at the man behind her. He is wiry, unshaven, with a tense edginess in his eyes.

"I'm just trying to find room to breathe," he responds. "If you could just give me a bit of space."

"We're all as cramped as you are. Some of us just show more consideration," Jennifer retorts. We all avert our eyes in an effort to seem neutral.

Neal is the only one who has a bit more space to move. That's because he hasn't bathed in over a week, which is common for him. Those nearest him hold their breath for as long as they can.

I almost don't notice Laura, who has been separated from the group. Her glasses are fogging up and she looks flushed. John is so tall he looms over the rest of us. He is furtively staring at Laura, then quickly looking away. It's like he has calculated how long he can maintain his gaze before it can technically be called leering.

Although it already seems impossibly crowded, more people manage to force their way in at each stop. With the congestion comes an increase in tension. Humans are not meant to be packed together like this. It turns us all into misanthropes. I'm feeling increasingly stifled and somewhat panicky. I decide to get off several stops early and walk the rest of the way home.

As I'm ascending the stairs of the subway station, I pass Rebecca descending. She has the same giant Slurpee in her hand. She doesn't seem to notice me.

A sense of euphoria envelops me when I step into the open air on the street. About a block from the subway station, I pass Parker and Laura engaged in conversation. They don't seem to notice me either.

Then I see Parker selling hand sanitizer outside a boarded-up shoe store. Again, she doesn't seem to notice me.

When I get home, I find Sandy doing email at her desk. She looks up with a smile. I ask about her day and she says it was a productive day with several virtual meetings. I tell her that I'm going to have a shower to revive myself before dinner. I feel restored by the steamy water on my back. Then I hold my breath and turn my face into the full force of the shower. After toweling off, I fall naked onto our bed to luxuriate in the warmth and ease of being home.

I am a bit startled to see Sandy walk into the bedroom, also naked. The light from the late afternoon sun through the bedroom window plays across her breasts. I have already developed an erection. Sandy mounts me and lowers herself onto my penis. She leans forward over me so that her ample hair hangs in my face. I struggle not to choke on her hair as she begins riding me up and down. With each descent she seems to become heavier to the point that it is oppressive. I feel like the air is being pumped out of me like a bellows.

I am relieved when the sex is abruptly interrupted by someone ringing the front doorbell. Sandy looks at me apologetically, her hair now dripping with sweat. She dismounts and slips into the washroom. I scramble to my feet, throw on gym shorts and an old T-shirt. I rush downstairs to see who is at the door.

Neal has shown up to accompany me to our rec league baseball game. He is distressed to see that I'm not ready to go. "I'm so sorry. I completely forgot. Give me five minutes to dress and grab my glove."

The baseball diamond is next to a quarry about three kilometres away. Once I've changed into my baseball attire, we start running toward the park. I'm very quickly winded and gasping for air. I'm wondering if I may be ill because a run of this length wouldn't normally be a problem for me. I can't seem to draw any air into my lungs. But we arrive in time and I just need a few minutes to catch my breath.

It proves to be a good game as much as these rec league games can be. We are ahead by one with two out in the bottom of the ninth. Reynolds is pitching. The opposition batter hits a sharp liner to Jennifer, who bobbles the ball and throws too late to Parker on first. The next batter hits a long one to right field that sends John running but it clears the fence. It's actually so well struck that it lands somewhere in the neighbouring quarry. I jump the fence to see if I can track it down. I quickly see the spot where it landed and realize that the ball has dropped into a pit about the size of a shipping container. I clamber down into the pit to retrieve the ball.

Stuffed Animals

• • •

I am vaguely aware of the sounds of laboured breathing from those around me. Hopeful inhalations followed by exhalations of despair. Soon, no matter how hard I listen, it is only my own breath I hear.

WORDS I HAVE
NOT SPOKEN

DIAMOND

IT WAS TWO DOWN IN the top of the ninth. The score was tied at two runs apiece. Casey was on the mound as she had been throughout the game. There really wasn't another pitcher that could be trusted with the ball when the championship was on the line. She worked the batter to a full count and then got a called strike with a slider low and inside.

In the bottom of the ninth there was a ground out at first and a soft pop fly caught by the second baseman. Casey was the third batter up and she found a hole in the infield to the left of the shortstop. On the next pitch she stole second.

Coach Tom stared intently at her. He seemed agitated but that was understandable since the team was poised to win their first Peewee championship. It was more than that, though. It was her young, tanned thighs as she took a lead off second base and knowing that he wouldn't have her around after this game.

The next batter hit a solid single to right field, which allowed Casey to score from second.

The team mobbed her as she crossed home plate. As the group dispersed with sweaty high-fives, Tom embraced Casey. "Way to go, girl! You were amazing."

Tom had an inspiration as the girls gathered their equipment in the dugout. "Team, to celebrate our championship, I'm going to take you on a daytrip to the beach next Saturday. I'll be in touch with your parents. Congratulations. Great job!"

Tom rented the school bus that they always used for their away games and the girls met at the ballpark. They drove to Lake Huron and had a day swimming and playing beach volleyball. Toward the end of the afternoon as it was getting close to the scheduled time to drive back to the city, Tom approached Casey and asked her to walk up the beach with him. He said he had something for her. They walked in the sand, talking about Casey's upcoming family vacation. Then Tom suggested they sit for a moment. He commented on the sun sparkling off the waves as they pulsed into shore. Then he reached into his pocket and pulled out a jewellery box. He said, "I didn't want to embarrass you by giving you this in front of the other girls but it is so obvious that you were our MVP I wanted to give you something as an award."

Casey opened the box to find a ring. She blushed and didn't know what to say. As they stood up, she stuffed it in the pocket of her shorts so that no one would know about it. Tom said, "Give me a hug, girl." Casey wanted nothing more than to get away from Tom, to be back with the other girls, to be on the bus home, but she felt she had no choice but to return his embrace. She didn't say a word on the walk back to the parking lot.

ICE

Casey wasn't as strong in hockey as she was in baseball but she loved the speed of the game. They were playing in Shaunavon against the Badgers early in February. They lost the game but Casey came away with an assist so she felt good about her effort. At the end of the game the small group of friends and family were leaving the arena when Casey spotted her old baseball coach, Tom, sitting by himself in the stands. She skated directly to the dressing room.

The girls had carpooled and Casey had been paired with the goaltender, Hailey. Hailey's dad drove them to Shaunavon in his SUV. Casey changed quicker than Hailey so she waited for her outside the arena. She kept watching to see if Tom would come out of the arena but she really hoped to avoid him. Had he somehow known that she would be there that evening?

Hailey and Casey loaded their gear into the car and set off for the city. They were halfway home, on Concession 6, when the car hit a slick patch on the frozen road and collided with a fencepost. Hailey immediately developed a goose egg on her forehead from where she hit the dash, but otherwise everyone was unharmed. The car was stuck against the post on a snowy embankment so Hailey's dad called CAA for a tow.

They were all shaken up and beginning to feel the cold when a car pulled over on the road next to them. It was Tom. Casey introduced him to Hailey and her dad. Tom offered whatever help might be needed but Hailey's dad explained that he was waiting for a tow. Tom turned to Casey and said, "Well, there's no need for you to wait. I can take you home." Casey looked imploringly at Hailey and her dad but was unable to articulate a reason to decline his offer.

Tom had only driven a short way when he pulled over. He said "Casey, it just occurred to me I've got just the thing to calm your nerves."

He had a small cooler in the backseat. He prepared a drink in a plastic cup and handed it to Casey, saying, "Virgin sidecar, on the rocks. Cheers!"

LAW

Casey worried obsessively about the incident for about a week before she reached out for advice. A friend of her mother's was a social worker, so Casey asked to talk to her. Sitting in the woman's home office she looked nervously at the plants and family photos adorning the space. Then she explained what had happened on the drive back from Shaunavon.

"I really don't know what happened. I don't know if anything happened. All I know is that he woke me in his car outside our house. When I got inside I found out that instead of it being about six o'clock, which I would have expected, it was close to eight o'clock. It makes no sense."

The woman looked intently in Casey's eyes before finally asking, "Do you trust this man?"

"No, I don't. But what should I do? Should I call the police? I can't say that, like, a crime was committed or anything."

"Well, I'm not an expert in this sort of thing, Casey, but I'm really glad you've decided to talk to me about it. I have to say, I don't think the police would take this very seriously."

"But what if he's, like, a known sexual predator? Shouldn't the police know so that other girls can be protected?"

"I know what you mean, Casey, but I think the best thing we can do is think about your own health and safety. I could refer you to a therapist, if you think that would help. But I wouldn't say a word to the police."

SNOW

Casey's parents went to Hamilton to visit Casey's grandmother. A blizzard unexpectedly swept through the area and, around nine o'clock, Casey got a call from her dad to say that, due to the inclement weather, they felt it was best to stay in Hamilton overnight.

Generally Casey didn't mind being home alone but she had been feeling uneasy ever since the incident with Tom. She felt particularly nervous now that he knew where she lived. The ice-encrusted bushes outside the living room creaked against the window, adding to her unease.

She checked the locks on the front and back doors before going to her room to connect with friends on social media.

Tom had been making more regular use of cocaine over the last few months, leading to increasingly erratic behaviour. One result of this is that he lost his job as a business analyst with Home Depot. He did a line of cocaine the night of the blizzard and the onrush of energy gave him the inspiration to walk the five kilometres to Casey's house. He had no idea what he would do when he got there but he had been obsessed with the idea of going back there since the night he dropped her off.

A walk that would ordinarily take about an hour took closer to three hours due to the wintry conditions. By the time he arrived on her street the effects of the cocaine had long since worn off. His feet were cold and wet and he was feeling irritable.

Casey decided to check the locks once again before going to bed. When she went to the front door she pulled a chair over and looked out the lunette above the door. She was immediately filled with fear as she saw a man standing in front of the house looking her way. She couldn't swear that it was Tom but he was wearing the same Home Depot toque Tom had had on the night he drove her home.

She fell into a panic and didn't know what to do. She opted to pull a sleeping bag into the bathroom and make a bed in the tub so that she could be behind one additional locked door. She was still there when her parents arrived home the next morning.

SOUND

A teacher at Casey's school who was assigned to monitor the hallways approached a man who had entered the school by a door near the gym that should have been locked. The teacher recognized right away that the man had mental health or substance abuse issues. When asked what he was doing in the school, he claimed he had to get his daughter from class due to a family emergency. The teacher explained that there were procedures that had to be followed. He invited the man to accompany him to the office, where his identity could be confirmed. The man refused to go to the office or to produce any ID. He finally agreed to leave. The teacher escorted him out the front door of the school but then waited in an alcove in the hallway. Sure enough, after ten minutes, the man was back inside the school. This time, the teacher was more assertive. He ordered the man to leave and said he was calling the police.

The teacher reported all of this to the principal.

The police arrived to find the man still on school property. They spoke to him and, after determining that he was not an immediate threat to anyone, let him go with the warning that he would be charged the next time he ventured onto school property. As he left the schoolyard, Tom pocketed a rubber ball that had been abandoned after some recess game. The minor theft felt like some form of retribution.

Casey left school at the end of the day with one of her friends. They walked together most of the way but then separated to reach their respective homes. Casey's route took her through a wooded area where she would never go when it was dark but there was still an hour or so of light left in the winter's day.

As she walked through the patch of forest, she heard a branch snap behind her. She turned to find herself facing Tom. She should have bolted for home but she was caught off guard. Tom said, "Casey, what a nice surprise to run into you here. I've been missing you lately. You know, you've always been special to me. Can I take you for a drink somewhere?"

Casey started to move away but Tom grabbed her by the arm and pulled her against him. "Casey, I need you to stay with me for a while. You'll do that for me, won't you? And you won't say a word."

BOMBER

God delivered the following instructions to Dzokhar.

"Your task is to find The Angel. You will need three pieces of information. Each piece will be given to you at the gateway to death."

• • •

In his teens, Dzokhar decided he would set his aspirations on being a featherweight boxer. He joined a local gym and began training obsessively. While his hands were quick and he had no lack of passion, he wasn't able to grasp the subtleties of the sport. Despite the trainers' repeated instructions, he failed to learn how to pace himself or defend himself. One day, while Dzokhar was sparring, a trainer kept telling him to use his left jab, but Dzokhar, impatient for big results, kept throwing a right cross that missed wildly every time. Finally, the trainer snapped and yelled, "Are you deaf or stupid?"

Dzokhar jumped out of the ring and went after the trainer. Other fighters held him back. After he calmed down, the trainer suggested he take some time away from the gym to work on his general conditioning. He suggested running. Dzokhar felt disrespected and never returned to the gym.

When Dzokhar heard that his Uncle Mike was in intensive care, dying of a gunshot wound to the abdomen, he immediately took a bus to the town where his uncle was hospitalized. He found Mike in pain but clear-headed. He told Dzokhar about the incident.

"It's so stupid. I was at Jack's place watching Formula One and, over the course of the evening, I'd had too much to drink. I was walking home afterward and passed by this house that had a chicken coop at the side. I don't know why but with my judgement impaired by alcohol, I decided to liberate the chickens. I was undoing the latch when the owner appeared out of the house with a .410 bore shotgun. After some yelling and posturing, he shot me in the belly. Can you image the humiliation of dying from a .410 for tampering with a chicken coop?"

Mike died two days later. He left behind his business as an independent contractor doing parging and other minor renovations. Knowing Dzokhar's life was lacking direction, Mike's widow suggested that Dzokhar take on the business. Dzokhar initially bristled at the idea, thinking it was too menial, but he really had no other options.

• • •

Dzokhar met Shannon on the beach near the marina. He was immediately struck by her beauty, but that was something he could not acknowledge, even to himself. What he did avow was that he was impressed with how modestly she was dressed compared to the other expats on the beach.

Shannon complained about her job and Dzokhar said he could hire her. Shannon wondered how he could make that impulsive assertion without knowing anything about her skills or experience, but she was in a phase of her life where she was willing to take a chance on any opportunity that presented itself. She took the job of Dzokhar's personal assistant at his import/export business. It wasn't long before they were sleeping with each other, and soon Shannon had moved into his apartment.

While initially Dzokhar didn't seem to care whether Shannon did any work at all, he grew increasingly critical of her efforts. He would snap at her for failing to relay messages from clients or even for neglecting to keep a fresh pot of coffee available in the office. The first time he actually struck her was enough for her to decide to move out. When she told him that, the assault was more severe. She suffered bruises on her face and arms. She recruited a friend and the friend's brother to accompany her when she went to the apartment to pack up her things. Dzokhar swore at her throughout the process.

Dzokhar read a newspaper account of an honour killing in upstate New York. A father and two brothers took a young woman to a remote lake, killed her with a hunting knife, and disposed of her body in the lake. They had long objected to how she dressed but the final straw was when they suspected her of having premarital sex. Dzokhar felt indignant anger, not about the killing but about the young woman's wanton behaviour.

Dzokhar took a large hunting knife and a spool of nylon rope to the home of an immigrant family. He arrived in the early evening. Threatening the members of the family with the knife, he said he would tie their hands and then leave them unharmed after he selected items of value from the home. He followed through with tying the hands of the husband and wife, the wife's father, who lived with them, their son, and two daughters. Then he sat in an armchair in the living room and admired his work for almost an hour. He showed no interest in looking for items of value. Then he dispassionately cut the throat of the father, followed by the old man and the twelve-year-old son. He left the house empty-handed.

When Dzokhar was developing and testing his bombs, he made a point of purchasing pressure cookers and garage door openers one at a time from different hardware stores in the city. The items themselves are innocuous enough, but he was concerned that repeated purchases of the same items might raise concerns.

• • •

So many people running toward, running toward. They're like salmon swimming upstream. But unlike salmon, it only takes one deliberate intervention and then they are running away from.

• • •

They took the Red Line to Central Station and then walked from there. They walked up Prospect to Cambridge, then down Cambridge to Norfolk. They found the humble clapboard house at 410.

The front door was unlocked, so they entered without knocking. They walked together through empty rooms until they found the angel in the master bedroom. He was dressed entirely in black, huddled in the closet, looking terrified.

• • •

Dzokhar was so reviled that no cemetery was willing to accept his remains. Finally, they negotiated an agreement with an Indigenous community in the northwest to inter him in their sacred burial grounds in exchange for a moratorium on the shipment of crude oil through their unceded territory. The grave was not marked in any way.

THE JUGGLER

I didn't hate school, but on occasion I went to bed hoping I would come down with the flu so that I could have a sick day. On this particular evening I got an ice cube from the freezer and rubbed it on the back of my neck, naively thinking the freezing cold would give me a fever, but I woke up the next morning feeling as healthy as ever. I decided to resort to the alternate plan of lying to my mother. I told her I wasn't well and would have to stay home from school. She took my temperature and, although it was normal and I'm sure she saw through my ruse, she decided to grant me a day at home. I didn't play that stunt very often.

I stayed in bed reading comic books about superheroes and super villains who I found equally appealing. There were characters like the Silver Surfer and Doctor Octopus. I could read the same issues over and over. Eventually I started feeling restless and a little guilty, so I decided to seek alternative amusements in the den. On the way there, my mother asked how I was feeling. I assured her that I was already starting to feel better. "Probably just a twenty-four-hour thing." I think that was an expression I'd heard on TV.

The den was my favourite room in the house and it was partly because of the distinctive wallpaper. It was a midnight blue with silvery moons and suns interspersed with arabesques. I think it was very old but well preserved.

In the den we had a set of *Encyclopaedia Britannica* that could absorb my attention for hours. In those pre-internet days it seemed like we had the entire scope of human knowledge stored on a single shelf. Thinking back on it now, I wonder about my parents' decision to buy the encyclopedia, a sizable purchase. Did they see it as an investment in their children's education? Or was it a product of the time that every middle-class home was expected to have a set of encyclopedia?

I pulled out a volume at random and, after skimming some entries about Japan and jellyfish, I found my attention was drawn to an entry on juggling. It included a brief introduction to a basic juggling technique. I grabbed a few sponge balls from our toy bin in the basement and then tried to follow the instructions. After struggling for several minutes, I finally managed to get one ball from my right hand to my left hand before dropping the other two balls. But then I stopped. A chill came over me and I had the eerie sense that someone was watching me. I turned around and saw a woman standing quietly in the corner. She was wearing a full-length skirt and a shawl that made her look like she'd stepped out of one of the historical photographs in the encyclopedia. I should have panicked but there was something immediately reassuring about her. Then she spoke to me with a voice that seemed to emanate from the bottom of a well.

"When you are learning to juggle, your hands are confused because they are tossing and catching at the same time. One hand is demanding your attention for one act while the other is sending a contradictory message. You cannot focus on one to the detriment of the other. It is like a fusion of opposites. Tossing and catching need to feel like one unified activity. When you play the piano, your hands are in two different staves. Only when you think of it as one song are you able to perform."

She coached me for the better part of an hour, by which time I was actually getting quite good at it. Then my mother called me for lunch. The woman gave me a conspiratorial smile and then seemed to twinkle before disappearing into the wallpaper.

I was eager to demonstrate my new skill to my mother, but I never mentioned my juggling tutor. I'm not sure why. It just seemed like something very private and personal.

My mother, commenting on my elevated energy, humoured me by saying, "I find you never appreciate your health so much as just after you've recovered from an illness." I sheepishly agreed with her.

• • •

I maintained my interest in juggling over the years, often using it to entertain my nieces and nephews at family gatherings. I have a brother with two sons and a sister with three daughters. I have never been married but I love my extended family. Still, my mother was always my biggest fan. Sometimes I thought she was more proud of me for my juggling than she was of the fact that I'd gone to graduate school and landed a good job with the federal government.

My mother stayed on alone in the house where we had lived as a family until declining health forced us to move her into a nursing home. My siblings and I had many anxious conversations, but because I lived closer to her, it fell to me to deal with most of the logistics. Plus, I had banked some sick days that could be used as needs arose. When the time came, my mother's move to the nursing home was abrupt. A vacancy opened up and we needed to act quickly. In contrast, getting the house ready for sale was a painfully slow process.

The day I took her to the nursing home, my mother and I spent some time compiling a list of things that she wanted from the house. She didn't need much and couldn't really accommodate a lot in her new setting, but some familiar pictures on the walls and decorative items on a shelf would be reassuring. There were some family portraits and one painting by a friend of the family that was quite awful but my mother had always loved it. She had a passion for dogs and had accrued a collection of ceramic dogs that meant a lot to her. Once we completed the list, I went back to the house to pull things together for her.

It felt like some form of violation to be in the house where I grew up after just extracting the woman who had raised me. In all my years growing up there, I rarely had the house to myself. I spent a long time wandering from room to room without attending to the task that brought me there.

I knew that some of what had belonged to me in my youth had been stored in the basement, including some old crates filled with vinyl LPs. I went down to the pitch-black basement, pulled the familiar string to switch on the bare lightbulb, and dragged some crates into the light. I leafed nostalgically through the LPs, many bringing back poignant memories while some I couldn't recall ever having seen before. I picked out a Joni Mitchell album and took it upstairs to my mother's stereo. I hadn't heard it in decades.

He says, "Big bird dragging its tail in the dust.
Snake kite flying on a string."

Something about this merging of earth and sky made me think of my juggling angel from those many years before. On a hunch I took a few balls to the den and put them to use. Almost immediately I felt the chill of an unnatural presence.

"You have become quite proficient over the years. It is good to see."

Sure enough, the woman appeared in the same corner of the room. I saw her differently as an adult than I had as a child. She seemed quite young, maybe in her mid-twenties. Her wardrobe seemed to reflect both poverty and dignity.

"How in the world do you recognize me? I think I was about eight years old the last time I saw you."

"Oh, I have kept my eye on you and your family over the years. I will miss your mother."

I didn't know how to respond and just watched her fade away. The pattern of the wallpaper started to show through her until that was all there was to see.

• • •

My plan had been to work until I retired with a full pension at age sixty-five, but my stage four colon cancer was making it clear that I'd have to adjust my expectations. The cancer had been diagnosed two years earlier but had already metastasized and was spreading quickly. I was staying on long-term sick leave while knowing I would never return to work.

The thought came to me that one thing I'd like to do, while I still could, would be to see the old house one last time. It had been twenty years since my mother had moved out and we'd sold the house. Not knowing who owned it now, I opted to leave a note in their mailbox explaining my situation. Driving up that familiar street and ascending the steps to the front porch had my heart pounding painfully. The new owners kindly contacted me within a couple of days and said they'd be delighted to have me over for tea some afternoon and give me a chance to look around. They warned me, however, that they'd made a lot of changes to the house and they didn't want me to find that upsetting. We made plans for the following Saturday afternoon. On a hunch, I brought along a few of my juggling balls.

At the appointed time I returned to the house and, for the first time in my life, rang the doorbell and waited to be let in. I was greeted by a young man who introduced himself as Dave. Then I met his wife, Jessica, their four-year-old daughter, and their baby son.

It was quite a shock to see the house. Nothing seemed quite the way I remembered it. Where I remembered natural wood that seemed to capture the family warmth, the house was now dominated by stainless steel. They had ripped out most of the old wallpaper and completely remodeled the kitchen. I had to resist the temptation to criticize their arrangement of the furniture. "That's not where the sofa belongs!" That sort of thing.

Fortunately, the den was much the same as I remembered it, including the old wallpaper. I asked if I could have just a few moments alone there to say goodbye to my memories. They could tell this was an emotional experience for me and urged me to take as much time as I needed. I looked to where the encyclopedia used to sit. Then I scanned the wallpaper in anticipation of her appearance. I took out my balls and began juggling. As I hoped, the woman showed up, accompanied by the now familiar chill in my bones.

Apologetically I said, "I'm afraid my skills have deteriorated. I don't have the dexterity I once had."

"It is a natural result of growing old," she replied. "At least, that is what I understand. I never had the privilege myself."

I stopped juggling and turned my full attention to her. She looked just as I remembered her, wearing the same clothes, not having aged at all. "You know, I feel like I've known you my whole life, but I know nothing about you. Tell me about yourself."

"Well, as you might have guessed, I grew up in this house. My father owned an apothecary nearby. In my teens I became enamoured with vaude-ville and decided to develop my art as a juggler. I performed locally under the stage name of Dawn Nightshade. My act was minor, easily overshadowed by the singers, dancers, and comedians, but it was an exciting experience for me. My career ended when I got involved with a stagehand and became pregnant out of wedlock. My parents were understandably mortified. They opted to keep me confined to the house until the child was born. It was a son. But I died in childbirth and was never able to give him a mother's love."

My eyes welled up with tears as I thought she seemed a child herself at that moment.

"Thank you, Dawn Nightshade. I should go. I don't want to abuse the hospitality of my hosts."

I thanked Dave. He said I should feel free to return if I ever felt the need, but I think he knew I never would. As I left the house I saw Jessica with their daughter on the front lawn. The little girl was tossing a ball in the air and catching it.

GOLEM

When I designed the golem I wanted to make him as generic as possible. I say "him," but his gender was ambiguous. I made him slightly shorter than most men so he would attract less attention. He had no identifiable ethnicity. My thinking was that if he were as nondescript as possible he would fit in everywhere. I worry that my decisions have had the opposite impact.

I had been struggling to find soil with which to make the golem because we have almost no arable soil in the country. Then my friend Ainsley told me about the experimental garden where they were having success growing artichokes. She told me it was rumoured that the garden was irrigated with the tears of the homeless.

I slipped into the garden in the middle of the night and removed a small bucket of soil from among the sprouting artichokes. A small amount was all I needed and it wouldn't be missed. For the rest of the golem I could use clay from the northern region.

The day I released the golem I followed him up the street and it was typical of so much of his subsequent experience. He was approaching a woman with two young children. When the woman spotted the golem, she stopped and turned to avoid him. Then a group of four people who were engaged in conversation fell silent when he approached. They watched suspiciously as the golem passed by. A few doors up the street he happened upon an elderly woman who had collapsed by her back door. He knelt beside her to see if she was OK and to help her back to her feet. But then the four people he had passed earlier showed up. One of them shouted, "Leave that poor woman alone!" The others shoved him away as the woman looked around in confusion.

There was a young man with schizophrenia who was known among shop-keepers downtown. He spent his nights in an alley beside the post office. During the day he would wander around, seeking shelter when he needed it, generally being reasonable and harmless. There were times, though, when his behaviour was more erratic and he would be encouraged to move on so as not to scare away the shoppers. One evening in the fall when the nights were getting colder, the golem happened upon him in his makeshift home in the alley. Without warning the golem ripped away his sleeping bags and blankets and began kicking him forcefully. When the young man stood up, the golem struck him across the side of the head, knocking him back down. The young man then clambered away as quickly as he could, leaving all his belongings behind.

That incident signalled a dramatic change in the golem's behaviour. His days were spent seeking out encampments that the homeless had established. He would tear them down and chase the residents away, resorting to physical violence when necessary. He took pride over the neighbourhoods that had been cleansed of street people.

An opinion piece ran in the city newspaper vilifying the golem for his treatment of homeless people. That was followed by a letter from a reader pointing out that the golem himself was homeless.

Amongst his colleagues, Constable Cann was known to praise the golem. "You know, he's cleaning up our downtown more effectively than we can because he doesn't have to worry about bylaws or public opinion." And yet when Constable Cann encountered the golem, he would berate him and threaten him. He even tazed him on one occasion. The golem was terrified of Constable Cann.

The golem found a sheet of corrugated metal at a construction site and dragged it into the woods by the river. He secured it to a half-fallen elm tree to create a serviceable shelter. He managed to spend three nights there before Constable Cann showed up at dusk on the fourth night. Cann chased him away with a blow from his truncheon and threw the metal into the river. The golem was left to cobble together a new home.

As winter set in, a group of the homeless decided to reclaim some of their turf. They moved through the alleys at night and began setting up their make-shift shelters with tarp and sleeping bags. When the golem realized what was happening, his response was ruthless. He chased them out before they could gather their meagre belongings. Several of them sustained injuries and one young man was actually killed when he fled into the path of a city bus. Once they were removed, the golem gathered up the remnants of their shelters and burned them all in a dumpster.

Spontaneous protests in support of the homeless began developing throughout the city. This took the form of peaceful gatherings in most cases but also involved the blocking of traffic and, later at night, fires and looting. The general anger and indignation put pressure on the police to take some form of action.

Constable Cann captured the golem under the North Wellington Bridge. Because he wasn't human, no warrant for his arrest was required, nor were formal legal proceedings deemed necessary. He was taken to the city incinerator. I was called in to assist with the process. As I had created him it was believed the golem would trust me. I was instructed to tell him that the incinerator was a health facility where he would be checked for communicable diseases. I could tell he knew I was lying but by that point he felt so defeated that he walked willingly into the incinerator. He had no will to argue or resist. He was burned alive. His ashes were then buried in the clay soil north of the city.

THE RIVER

In memory of Tracy

"There was once a warrior princess who did battle with an invincible dragon. Every day she would paddle up the river to confront him. Sometimes she managed to hold the dragon at bay; other times she returned from her foray weakened and wounded. But each new dawn she put her pain and fear aside and returned to the river. Eventually, she succumbed to the dragon's terrible fury."

"But why battle a dragon who could never be defeated?"

"Her reward is a river that runs stronger. It is fed by the tears of those who loved her."

COROLLA

The president's team had been preparing for the event for weeks. His suit was hand-tailored from the finest cashmere and silk blend and complemented with a designer floral tie. His makeup was applied with the artistry of an Italian fresco. Lighting for the podium was developed with the care befitting a Broadway play. Every detail was considered to ensure he would be presented in the most flattering way possible. He stepped confidently into the spotlight with that smile his coaches had nurtured for maximum influence.

"Good evening, ladies and gentlemen. Thank you for taking time from your busy schedules to be here for this auspicious occasion. As you know, tonight I am here to announce the winner of the President's Medal for Peace and Human Rights. This is the most historic and prestigious award in the world."

From a table to the president's left, a reporter with the *Garden City Expositor* was heard commenting, "You only established the award last year."

Seated next to the president was an attractive young blonde woman named Rose Dixon. She held the position of presidential aide and director of communications. The president leaned toward Rose, out of the spotlight, and gave her a directive. "Have that man escorted out." Rose sent a text to a member of the security detail and then watched as the reporter was taken by the elbow and led from the room.

The president continued. "The award honours the individual anywhere in the world who has made the greatest contribution to human well-being and dignity. Far too often these advocates for a better world toil in anonymity. Driven by their own passion for justice, they work tirelessly on behalf of the poor and downtrodden, members of society who cannot represent themselves. I have to say, we have never had a more deserving recipient than the man we are honouring this evening. He single-handedly eliminated war, hunger, and corruption in the Middle East. I am so proud to announce that my own son, Paul, has been selected to receive the 2021 President's Medal for Peace and Human Rights!"

Applause from the audience was aborted when the vice president, seated at the head table, interrupted the president. With a look of mortification on his face, he said, "I'm sorry, Mister President, but it is your other son, Mark, who you appointed special envoy to the Middle East."

The president's efforts to maintain a facade of good humour gave way to irritation at being publicly corrected. He returned his attention to Rose. "Make a note. We will initiate impeachment proceedings against the vice president on Monday."

Recovering his demeanour of confidence and bravado, he returned his attention to the audience. "I have always been dedicated to nurturing the highest values in my children and so it is with great pride that I give this recognition of how Paul has blossomed into a true hero for human rights."

The president's equanimity was again dispelled when a man with a darker complexion stood up at the back of the room. "This is outrageous! Your administration has overseen genocide in the Middle East on an unprecedented scale! You should be ashamed to utter the words *human rights*."

Several members of security, not waiting for orders, pounced on the man and dragged him outside. Meanwhile, the president turned once more to Rose. "I need you to draft a new executive order closing the border to anyone from Arabic or Muslim countries. Have it on my desk first thing Monday morning."

His face flushed with irritation, the president decided to cede the podium to another speaker. "I will now call on the former secretary of defense, Charles Aster, to say a few words about our accomplishments in the Middle East." The president added smugly, "I issued a presidential pardon so that Charles could be here with us today. Charles?"

"Thank you, Mister President. Yes, we should all be very proud of what our country accomplished under the president's leadership. It is important to understand that we need to look beyond the surface appearance portrayed by the media. Yes, innocent people were killed, communities were destroyed, but to meet our goals we needed to pull evil out by its roots. If we were constrained by surface appearances, evil would grow back stronger than ever."

At that moment, anger flashed across the president's face as he caught sight of an orchid on the table just to his left. Glaring at Rose, he complained, "What is that orchid doing here? I told you I am allergic to orchids!"

Rose patiently responded, "But Mister President, it's not a real orchid. It's artificial."

The president paused for a moment, then turned back to Rose. "Of course it is, but that doesn't matter. It's a question of principle. An orchid is an orchid and I said no orchids. Clear out your desk on Monday. We'll offer your position to that young woman from the policy office. What's her name? Lily?"

LEFT

I saw a poster advertising a talk on the ouster of the socialist president. There were some members of society who referred to it as a coup orchestrated by foreign powers. Others claimed the president had rigged the last election and had been silencing opposition. Although I knew the organization hosting the talk was highly cynical about the current government, I felt it would be useful to get first-hand exposure to the arguments. It was so hard to disentangle fact from politics in the media. I felt more confident about putting an individual speaker's bias in perspective.

As it turned out, the speaker was very engaging. I felt like an outsider as it was clear that most of the people in attendance were regular members. Much of the discussion after the talk was about how to mobilize society to participate in marches and demonstrations. I was really there to observe the dynamic and consider what side of the debate I was on.

I felt it necessary to be cautious. I wasn't looking to sign on with any organization or ideology, but I knew there were concerns about infiltrators, informants recruited by the state intelligence service to gather information and identify candidates for surveillance. I didn't want my ambiguity to be misinterpreted.

At the beginning of the evening there were about fifty people in the room. During the talk, about ten people departed at various points. By the time the Q and A component finished, twelve people remained. I was an unfamiliar face lingering at the end of the evening and someone approached to ask if I was interested in joining or volunteering. I was relieved that no pressure was applied after I declined.

On my walk home, my attention was drawn by a poster in the window of a community arts centre. It was advertising a recital by people who had taken a course in soft shoe dancing. They were encouraging people to come to the performance with the incentive that attendees might be inspired to take a dance course themselves. I was actually intrigued by the prospect but simultaneously amused by my proclivity for putting myself in situations where I would feel clumsy.

My reverie was interrupted when I felt someone's touch on my shoulder. I turned to see an attractive woman with close-cropped hair and circular glasses. I immediately recognized her as one of the people who had been at the talk. "I hope I'm not disturbing you. I noticed you at our event this evening and thought I'd introduce myself. Christine is my name."

"Yes, I thought I'd noticed you there. I'm not a member. I just thought I'd check it out, learn a few things. And it certainly was informative."

"I'm glad to hear that," Christine replied. "My partner, Michelle, is on the executive. She couldn't be at the meeting as she had to work. She tends bar at Pimblett's. I was just going there to wait for her shift to end, if you'd like to come along for a pint."

As I sat with Christine over a pint I grew increasingly attracted to her. She was a beautiful woman with a warm and engaging personality. Eventually, Michelle was done at the bar and came over to our table. Christine introduced us and explained that I'd been at the talk earlier that evening. I immediately sensed something disapproving in Michelle's reaction to me. Perhaps she sensed my attraction to Christine or perhaps she resented my voyeuristic attendance at the talk. As much as I tried to make a good first impression, I sensed that she didn't trust me.

Christine suggested we exchange numbers so she could let me know about any upcoming events. I stayed at the pub after they left to have a late bite as I hadn't yet had dinner. I ordered curried chickpeas on rice and thought about the evening. One never knows when an opportunity will present itself nor what the ramifications might be.

While I ate my dinner, my attention was drawn to a tennis tournament in Abu Dhabi on the bar television. I felt oddly reassured watching something as familiar as tennis broadcast from a location that was totally alien to me.

Later that week the government issued a decree that voting laws would be changed to institute one vote per household rather than a vote for every eligible citizen. Furthermore, any disputes within the household would be resolved by the male head of the household. This represented an attempt to roll back over a century of universal suffrage.

The next day I got a text from Christine about a protest on the square in front of the cathedral. It was believed that the church had lobbied for the legislative change, a further example of their historic suppression of women. I decided to go, selecting attire that I thought most befitting of the event. Once I arrived I noticed Christine and Michelle amidst the most vocal cluster of protesters. I opted not to approach them.

Everyone was surprised when the priest came out of the cathedral and joined with the protesters. I saw him interviewed by someone from an alternative television network but I didn't know what he said until I saw it on the news that night. "The church believes that everyone, regardless of gender, sexual orientation, race or religion, should have an equal voice in a democratic society. We stand in opposition to the new law."

That weekend I sent a text to Christine. "Saw you at the demonstration a few days ago. Good turnout. Sorry I didn't get to say hi. Would you like to grab a coffee sometime over the weekend?"

I got a response right away. "Sorry, but I am not feeling well this weekend. Can I see you next week, maybe Wednesday?" I agreed to the day but something about her response left me with a sense of unease. I groped around in the fridge for a beer but realized that I was out. I decided to return to Pimblett's for a pint.

Michelle was working behind the bar so I approached her and said, "I hear Christine is ill. I trust it's nothing serious."

Michelle reacted with a look of shock. Then she turned to her colleague and said, "Can you cover for me for a few minutes?" Turning to me she said, "Come with me. We need to talk." She then led me through the bar kitchen to the back alley.

"Christine didn't come home last night and I haven't heard from her. I believe she's been arrested. We may hear that she's been charged with treason. It's also possible she'll be held without charge and we'll never hear anything. If you've heard from her it means they've confiscated her phone and they're using it to bait her contacts. I would advise you to ignore anything you receive from Christine's phone."

It was my turn to be shocked. "I can't believe it. You don't seem to be as upset by this as I would have expected."

"Listen, Christine and I have known that being involved in the movement means you have to expect this sort of thing. Dabblers like you should be careful. You can easily get in over your head. I have to get back to work."

I went back in the pub and sat at a table in a dimly lit corner. I tried to make sense of what Michelle had told me. I also noticed that there was tennis on the television as there had been during my last visit. Every time I looked at the screen, there seemed to be some sort of dispute between a player and a linesman.

On my walk home, I was serenaded by the flight vocalizations of nightjars.

Despite my better judgement, I decided to test whether Michelle was telling me the truth. I thought it was equally likely that she was paranoid, or even that she was simply trying to discourage me from developing a relationship with Christine. On Wednesday, I texted Christine's phone number.

"I hope you're feeling better. You suggested getting together this evening. I'm game."

I got a response back. "Yes, I'm feeling much better. Thank you. How about 9:00 at Christie Pits? There's a cafe I like just down the street from the park." I agreed to the proposed time and place, but I planned to go there early and wait in hiding to see who actually showed up.

When I got to Christie Pits, I found it deserted. Being right next to the subway it's usually a very active place. And normally the park is lit up with flood lights after dusk but the only light was from the moon and the street lights along the southern edge of the park. I chose a spot on the hill behind the baseball diamond, sat on the grass, and waited.

My mind drifted back to when I used to play baseball and to one game in particular, when I was caught in a run-down between third and home. It was an anxious situation. Through a series of feints and starts, I tried to avoid being tagged while eliciting as many throws as possible in the hopes that one of the infielders would bobble the ball, enabling me to reach home.

I felt someone's touch on my shoulder.

LONEY

There is a central corridor running the length of the weather station. On the right are a bunk room, a lab, and a living room. On the left are an office, a washroom and the kitchen. The bunk room, with two sets of bunk beds, is available for scientists doing field research who might need a place to stay but Bill has had the place to himself for years.

In the lab, next to a large jar containing a narwhal fetus, Bill has set up grow lights to cultivate cherry tomatoes and leaf lettuce. The living room has a television with no reception but an extensive collection of video tapes. There is also a bookcase with books and other diversions such as jigsaw puzzles.

The kitchen is stocked with dry goods from the south as well as locally procured caribou and there is Arctic char in the freezer. Bill occasionally snares an Arctic hare or ptarmigan as a source of fresh protein.

• • •

The wind is particularly strong today. The building rocks on its pillars like a ship at sea. I always find this movement a bit unnerving. I feel the isolation and vulnerability more than ever at these times. My demons are kept at bay during the day when I have duties to perform, but at night I'm given to restless pacing.

I sort through the collection of videotapes and pull out a recording of the Stanley Cup playoffs from two years before. I've watched it before and I certainly know the results, but it is a diversion. It will be six weeks before they bring me a new assortment of tapes along with food and other provisions.

I make myself a mug of tea and sit in the La-Z-Boy to watch the hockey. The voices of the announcers have the familiarity of old friends. I recall listening to the same voices throughout my youth in the south. My brother and I spent many evenings watching hockey in the basement of our parents' home.

During intermission I go in the lab and tell Loney how the game is progressing. I could fast-forward through the intermission, but that would defeat the purpose; the whole challenge of life here is about filling the time. Loney favours the New England Whalers so he doesn't show much interest in this series between the Bruins and the Habs.

• • •

Once every three months Bill must rendezvous with a technician named Sprague so that they can exchange data tapes. Bill brings data from his weather station and Sprague brings data from his research station. The data is exchanged to provide off-site redundancy in the event of catastrophic events at one site or the other. They come from opposite directions to meet for a day at an outpost that is roughly the geographic midpoint. The meeting also provides the only direct human contact both men will have during each leg of their residencies.

Bill fills his backpack with supplies for the three-day journey along with the data tapes. He secures his sleeping-bag and the pack onto the snowmobile with bungee cords. He loads a back-up battery and spare spark plugs in the storage compartment. A minor mechanical failure can be lethal in this environment.

About an hour into the journey, Bill decides to follow the curve of the land westward onto the crest of a hill. As he rounds a large outcrop, he startles a small herd of muskox routing for lichen. The animals quickly disperse, but then merge together again as they gallop away.

• • •

As my snowmobile caresses the contours of the land, I grow increasingly excited for this rare contact with another person that has been so long in coming. To hear a voice that has not been recorded on a VHS tape. To shake hands and feel the warmth of human life.

I stop for lunch in a sheltered cove along the shore, known to me from previous trips to the outpost. I savour the cured caribou and the bread that I baked last week. The sun is dazzlingly bright, but I see more ominous skies awaiting me to the south.

I'm not sure I still know how to interact with another person. Every personality is complex and mercurial, easily impacted by what I may say or do with no malevolent intention, but just as likely to target me with reactions to factors unrelated to me. How is it ever possible to fully understand a single exchange with another human being?

• • •

There are minimal amenities at the unmanned outpost: two cots, a hotplate, a latrine, not much more.

A tradition has developed over the years that each man would bring something special from his larder to share in potluck fashion. On this occasion, Bill brings some smoked char and Swiss chocolate; Sprague brings an Arctic hare that he has snared and cured.

• • •

I am having a hard time dealing with Sprague. He has an unnerving habit of invading my personal space in a way that seems threatening, while, at the same time, being emotionally distant and inscrutable. I feel the need to be guarded while I'm here with him.

He seemed to find my contributions to our shared meal inadequate. And whenever I try to engage him in conversation, he reacts as though I have again failed to measure up to his expectations. I am constantly worrying that I have offended him. Perhaps my weeks of isolation have eroded my social skills. Or perhaps his own isolation has made him less tolerant of others. Or both.

Throughout last night, I could have sworn he was talking to other people. Of course, I imagined he was talking about me, complaining about me. Perhaps he was talking in his sleep. Or perhaps I was dreaming. Or both.

• • •

Having completed his sojourn at the outpost, Bill prepares for his journey back to the weather station. There is little sunlight at this time of year, but there is also little wind. Following the shoreline should get him there in under five hours; however, Bill is driving faster than normal and about five kilometres from the station his engine overheats. The snowmobile grinds to a halt and won't restart.

Recognizing that he is on the verge of losing the remaining daylight, Bill determines he is better off walking the rest of the way and returning the next day with enough daylight to sort out the problem.

The snow is dense and firm, allowing for relatively easy walking. He gets into a rhythmic, squeaky pace as his boots traverse the snow. The temperature drops as the night sets in but he arrives at the station before there is any risk of frostbite.

• • •

The tension with Sprague was becoming unbearable so I am relieved to be on my way back to the station. My departure was somewhat hasty without the usual checks to the snowmobile and other precautions. This leaves me uneasy and fearing some mishap.

As I ride north, my mind is churning over the awkward interactions with Sprague. Did I do something to offend him? Is he in fact angry with me? Or am I being oversensitive, even paranoid?

My snowmobile has suddenly seized up. I'm sure Sprague has sabotaged it. I recognize where I am and fortunately it should only take about an hour to complete the journey on foot. I move my pack from the snowmobile to my back and head off toward the station.

As I walk, I become increasingly anxious. I hear what sounds at first like growling, then an eerie sort of singing. Then, most unnerving of all, I'm sure I hear laughter. Although it doesn't make sense, I begin to see pairs of eyes shining in the darkness. I pick up my pace as I grow alarmed, but I don't want to exhaust myself before reaching the station. I spot a figure darting through the snow off to my left. I recognize Sprague. But how is it possible that he could be here? And why?

I break into a dead run when I finally spot the station. I am breathless when I unlock the door, slip inside, and secure the deadbolt behind me.

• • •

At the next day's first light, Bill gathers together some tools and hikes back to the snowmobile. After some inspection, he determines that the overheating has glazed the cylinders. He removes the cylinders and breaks the glaze with sandpaper. In a little over an hour, he has the engine running again and rides the snowmobile back to the station.

Bill takes some caribou out of the freezer to thaw in order to make a stew. Then from the bookcase in the living room he selects one of the few books he hasn't already read. He spends the afternoon reading a bestseller that was made into a successful movie.

Before starting work on the stew, Bill decides to do a little cleaning. He vacuums the corridor and living room and then cleans the porcelain in the bathroom. He changes the linens on his bed and throws the used linen in the laundry area.

• • •

I leave all the lights off to enable me to see into the darkness outside and to ensure I cannot be seen. I am at the kitchen window for almost an hour, my heart beating quickly, when I finally spot the first of them creeping toward the building. I cross to the window in the living room and immediately see another figure bent over, approaching cautiously. Then, behind him, I am sure that is Sprague.

I go to the corridor. Somehow I feel safer away from the exterior walls and windows. I sit on the floor, my arms around my knees. I listen. I study the thin, brown carpeting. I study the stains. I study the bits of debris missed by the vacuum. I wonder if there is evidence of meals I've eaten buried in the fibres.

The wind begins to pick up, creating a moan that permeates the building. The effort to remain intact causes the building's joints to creak. Then it becomes evident the invaders have surrounded the building. They are testing the deadbolt lock on the door. They are tapping on the windows. I think I can hear them calling out to me in tones that are both threatening and alluring.

I decide to get into bed without washing or even undressing. I know it is just a matter of time and there's nothing I can do about it. I lie there listening. Then I hear Loney emerging from his jar. I hear formaldehyde splashing to the floor. All the other sounds have stopped as if those outside are waiting. Loney makes his way down the corridor. I hear him releasing the deadbolt.

SAM KIRKWOOD

There are 800,000 people in the city. It might be interesting to get to know them one life at a time, one day at a time.

Let's start at the Cabaret Oscuro in Bourda. There's a man sitting alone at a table along the wall beneath a portrait of Queen Victoria. His name is Sam Kirkwood. He's sipping a pint of Fuller's ESB, dividing his attention between reading a novel and observing the other patrons. Particularly distracting is an animated conversation about gender transitioning. One person is looking forward to the next surgical procedure. No one seems concerned about being overheard. In fact, they seem to be enjoying the attention. One man has a toy magic wand and he is pretending to sprinkle fairy dust on the other patrons.

Sam's attention then falls on a woman who has just replenished her pint of beer at the bar. She has a fair complexion that contrasts sharply with her black hair. She is wearing a black, sleeveless T-shirt and army pants. She takes a sip of her beer and then, without a moment's hesitation, walks over to Sam's table as if it is where she naturally belongs. Only after sitting down does she ask, "Mind if I join you?"

Sam puts down his book and responds, "Not at all."

The woman rotates Sam's book so she can read the title. "*Orlando*. I haven't read that but I did see the movie. I've read other books by Virginia Woolf. I loved *A Room of One's Own*. I tried reading *Mrs. Dalloway*, but I couldn't manage it." She pauses for a moment and then says, "Saul."

Sam is momentarily confused before he realizes she is providing her name. But then he is unsure whether it is her first name or her last name. To be safe, he responds with his full name. "Sam Kirkwood. Nice to meet you."

"I felt like I was caught in a crowd, like Grand Central Station, and I was reading the thoughts of everyone who passed by me. But none of the thoughts connected to each other and I just felt confused."

Sam is wondering if this woman will always make him feel obtuse and befuddled. "Sorry?"

"*Mrs. Dalloway*. I'm talking about *Mrs. Dalloway*."

"Ah, yes. I'm sorry. To be honest, it mystified me the first time I read it, but after five years or so, I tried again and I made a stronger connection with it. What are you reading these days?"

"Actually, I don't read books anymore. I'm into zines. I'm drawn to zines with a social justice focus. Sex workers, mental health, the climate. Although I also have a weakness for fanzines."

"You know, I've never read a zine," Sam responds. Saul simply looks at him inscrutably. They end up having several drinks together. They share views on American politics, Banksy's art, endangered wildlife.

Then Saul announces she has to get home. Sam offers to walk with her. She says, "That would be nice. I'm just over at Brickdam and Winter."

As they walk, Sam senses Saul getting more distant. Perhaps she is just tired or perhaps she is trying to establish that she will not be inviting Sam in. In fact, when they arrive at her home she seems relieved when Sam doesn't stop with her but continues on his way. She calls out to him, "Hey, I'm going to a party on Friday. Would you like to come? There will be a lot of interesting people there." Sam says he would love that. He comes back so they can exchange numbers and then goes on his way with a bit more bounce in his step.

When the day of the party arrives, Sam decides not to reach out to Saul. He wants to be sure she really wants him to be there. That afternoon he gets a terse text from her. "The party is at Lot 3312 Princess Street. Any time after 9:00." He had been hoping for a bit more warmth and enthusiasm but he decides to keep an open mind.

It is closer to 10:00 when Sam arrives at the house on Princess Street. The last thing he wants is to arrive when the party is just getting started, and it would be painfully obvious that he doesn't know anyone. He enters the crowded and smoke-filled house prepared to explain his presence by saying, "I'm a friend of Saul." But no one pays him the least attention. The music that is playing at a high volume sounds like Throwing Muses. He finds his way to the kitchen, where he deposits his six-pack of beer, opening one. Then he goes back to the living room to scan the faces for Saul. He can't find her, but the more attention he pays to those in the room, the more convinced he is that there are a lot of hard drug users in attendance. Sam himself doesn't have any experience with drugs beyond marijuana.

After nursing his beer for about an hour, Sam decides to make his exit. There isn't anything about the experience that he is enjoying. He decides to take one more beer onto the back deck and enjoy the fresh air and relative quiet. Then he can leave from there without anyone noticing. Not that anyone would care whether he is there or not. He never did see Saul.

After what seems like an appropriate amount of time, Sam leaves his unfinished beer and exits through a gate into the back lane. He takes an alley back to the street and begins walking east, but he is barely a block away when he sees several police vehicles pull up in front of the house. Several officers run to the back whence he had made his exit moments before. Evidently the party is being raided and he left just in time.

Rather than risk being rounded up by the police, Sam decides to find somewhere he can be concealed until things calm down. He knows there is a graffiti-filled grotto under a bridge nearby and decides that might be the most appropriate place to take refuge.

When Sam arrives under the bridge he finds that someone else is there. He then recognizes Saul. She is wearing a shirt covered in Arabic writing.

"Saul, what are you doing here?"

"The same thing you're doing, I imagine."

"Were you at the party? I didn't see you there."

Saul responds with an explanation that doesn't really explain anything. "I was upstairs."

"Well, I'm glad you got out before the cops arrived. What's with the Arabic shirt?"

"It's Persian, actually. I'm reading 'the Shahnameh.'"

"I thought you only read zines."

"That was several days ago. Things change." Then Saul begins to move away. "Well, Sam Kirkwood, I have to go." Just before she ascends to street level, Saul turns back to Sam. "I'll re-read *Mrs. Dalloway*," she says. Then she's gone.

That's enough with Sam Kirkwood. Let's move on.

RESERVOIR

Patrick looked out over the reservoir, down toward the San Remo. The reflective water had a calming influence on him, like a balm to relieve the stress of the day. Lost in a meditative state, he was oblivious to the people passing behind him, running and/or pushing strollers. His attention was on the repetitive lapping of the water along the shore. But he felt something dark beginning to intrude. He looked down and felt disconcerted even before he recognized what he was seeing. The body of a drowned rat had settled on the shore's edge. Its mouth was locked open as though it had died with screams of agony. Patrick shuddered and turned away from the reservoir.

Heading east toward the Metropolitan Museum, he tried to recover his equanimity by focusing on the clouds drifting over 5th Avenue, but he was startled when someone stepped into his path. A gaunt man whose skin was darkened by too many hours in the sun stared into his eyes. Then he startled Patrick by blurting out, "Nickel or a dime or a penny or a quarter? Nickel or a dime or a penny or a quarter?" Patrick averted his eyes and took a wide arc to avoid him.

He went to the Metropolitan Museum, where he wanted to visit the book shop. He had in mind buying a book about the art of J.M.W. Turner. He had seen an image in which Turner depicted the sea with a dizzying violence. Patrick wanted to learn more about the man himself. After leafing through a coffee-table monograph, he concluded that it cost more than he was willing to spend. He asked a sales clerk, "Is this the only book you have on Turner?" She said it was. On the way out of the shop his eye was caught by a postcard reproduction of Jacques-Louis David's *Death of Marat*. In some ways, this was the polar opposite of Turner. With the carefully arranged elements lit like jewels in a display case, it came across more like a still-life painting than of a man murdered in his bath. And then Patrick thought about the French term for still life. *Nature morte.* Patrick bought the card and put it in the breast pocket of his jacket.

He decided that since it was a nice day and he had time to kill, he would walk all the way to his home in Chelsea. He had barely left the museum when he encountered a small group of protesters on 5th Avenue. From the signs they were carrying it was evident that they were drawing attention to the seemingly endless string of police killings of Black Americans. He paused to listen to their chant.

"What do we want?"

"Justice for Eric Garner!"

"When do we want it?"

"Now!"

Patrick listened to this call and response, like a mass for social justice, repeated with a series of victim names.

It seemed that society was becoming increasingly fractured. There was no end of problems to focus on and little hope for solutions. Patrick found it overwhelming. He preferred to focus on things that he could control. Effort should produce tangible results, like walking home, where one step after another got you closer to your goal.

Patrick thought about his passion for marathon swimming. It was different from walking, where your progress was evident, especially in New York City, where the descending street numbers confirmed the number of blocks you had traversed. Sometimes when swimming you could be struggling with a headwind or current and feel like all your effort is only enough to counter the forces that are pushing you away from your destination. In a situation like that, you have to concentrate on your stroke and trust that you are making progress.

He passed by the Lobster Club on 53rd and thought about the fact that everyone he knew seemed to love lobster but he wouldn't eat it. He'd sworn off lobster when his grandfather told him that the bodies of drowned fishermen, pulled off the ocean floor, would be covered in lobsters feeding on their flesh.

He approached Times Square and became aware of a large protest. Like the earlier event near the museum, the focus was on Black Lives Matter. He saw signs saying things like "I can't breathe" and "Say their names." As far as he could tell, there didn't seem to be any particular target of their protest.

Someone standing next to Patrick angrily muttered, "This sort of thing should be illegal."

"What's that?" Patrick asked.

"This, it's a huge public disturbance. The city is chaotic enough without this sort of nonsense."

Things seemed to be heating up between the police in riot gear and the protestors. Probably fearing looting, the police were setting up water cannons. Then they turned them on, indiscriminately breaking up the crowd. Patrick froze in disbelief when he saw a young girl knocked off her feet by the force of the water. Several people stumbled over her in their rush to escape. Finally, a man scooped her into his arms and carried her down the street. Patrick couldn't tell if she was conscious. He decided to swing north through Hell's Kitchen to avoid the Times Square area.

As the flashing lights and yelling were diminishing, so was his anxiety. A handmade BLM sign, carried by the wind, scuttled near his feet and settled in a puddle by the curb. He looked up at the sky as he walked and tried to be nourished by this moment of calm.

Near the Lincoln Tunnel, Patrick encountered yet one more crisis on the city streets. There were flashing lights and a small crowd had gathered. Patrick asked someone what was happening. "A man was hit by a Poland Spring truck. I think he was killed. This is the third time this year that someone has been hit here." It was only then that Patrick saw a splatter of blood on a New York Mets cap overlooked by the ambulance crew, lying in the gutter.

Patrick found himself in front of the West Club Bathhouse. Although it was only a few blocks from his home, he'd only been there once. It had been shortly after he and Alex separated and he had been trying various ways to meet someone new. A man he met there had told him that Gianni Versace's killer had been a member. Patrick never returned after that.

When he got home, Patrick pulled the postcard out of his pocket. He only now contemplated what he would do with it. He considered mailing it to a friend but it seemed like an odd sort of gift. He then remembered a book he had read in a French class in university. The title was *Les Dieux ont Soif* and it was about the French Revolution. It occurred to him that it was in that class that he had met his former lover, Alex. He and Alex had been on good terms since their relationship ended but he hadn't had contact with him for almost a year. Perhaps he would send the card to Alex.

Patrick turned the television on and found that reporters on the street had interrupted the mindless diversion that he was expecting. At first he thought they must be reporting on the conflict at Times Square but he soon realized it was something else. Apparently a man had been arrested for attempting to hack into the computer systems that control the city's water supply. His aim was to overload the water with a chemical that, at normal levels, played a benign role in killing pathogens. In the concentration that he attempted to release, the city's water would have been turned into poison. The reporter was outside the man's home in Washington Heights. He had been arrested there about an hour earlier. In addition to his computer equipment, a cache of weapons was discovered. He was apparently a veteran of the war in Iraq, had been working for one of the private security firms in the city, and it was rumoured that he had become involved in a neo-Nazi group.

The reporter closed with the assertion, "This represents an attempt at mass murder that violates all standards of human decency."

The phone rang. It was Patrick's friend Deborah. They had met when they were both graduate students doing research at the Columbia Water Center. She was calling to tell Patrick that her thesis advisor at the CWC, Ahmed Said, had just died. He had suffered a brain aneurysm two weeks prior. Deborah, in tears, said, "I've never known anyone who approached death with as much grace and dignity as Doctor Said."

Almost as soon as he hung up the phone, it rang again. This time it was his brother David in Brooklyn. David's son, Danny, had been in the hospital off and on for the past three months, battling cancer. Danny had celebrated his fourth birthday in the hospital. David said things had taken a turn for the worse. He suggested Patrick come to the hospital as soon as possible.

Patrick went immediately to the 23rd Street Station, where he caught the C Train for Brooklyn. He wasn't that close to his brother. They were civil to each other but had never really connected as adults. But Patrick adored Danny. He'd never really experienced a baby before Danny was born. Patrick had fallen in love with him immediately.

On the subway platform he saw two people carrying placards. One read, "Declare war on fracking. Protect our groundwater." The other read, "Oil industry reaping profits while the world dies of thirst."

When he arrived at the hospital room, David and his wife Carol were there. The destruction that the cancer and the chemo had wreaked on Danny were all too evident. His belly was distended, he looked emaciated and jaundiced.

Danny was desperately thirsty, but David and Carol weren't allowed to give him anything to drink. The most they could do was give him the occasional chip of ice to suck on. More fluid would further distress Danny's internal organs. He was pleading for another chip of ice. "Even just a little bit?"

Patrick couldn't take it anymore and he didn't want Danny to see him fall apart so he left the hospital quite abruptly. Although he'd already walked a lot that day, he decided he needed to walk off his grief and worry. He set off for the Brooklyn Bridge. On the way he passed the outdoor pool in Commodore Barry Park. He heard the children splashing in the pool, squealing with delight.

ISAAC

The instructions I received from his brother were to enter by the lane by the Presbyterian church. That lane would turn left and then left again. At the second turn I was to continue north on a footpath. The path would branch off to the right several times. On the third of these I would find Isaac's home. I really wasn't prepared for what I was entering. There was a great congestion of homes made up of dirt floors and whatever sheltering materials could be cobbled together. Sheet metal, plywood, cinder blocks. Nearly naked people of all ages watched me warily. The footpaths were squeezed so tightly between these makeshift homes that I could hardly walk without brushing up against them.

I asked an adolescent boy, "Do you know where Isaac lived?"

"Isaac is dead," he responded.

"Yes, I know that but I need to find where he lived."

The young man offered to show me. When I got there I found a young couple living there with a child. The young man, named Henry, claimed to be Isaac's cousin.

"We have been living with my parents. When we heard the sad news about Isaac, we knew that his place would be available. We have a bit of privacy now."

I explained that Isaac had buried something in the dirt floor of his home that he asked me to find and return to where it belongs. I asked Henry if he would mind if I tried to find it.

"How do I know you are here to serve Isaac's wishes? Perhaps you are just here to steal from us."

I reached into my satchel and pulled out a bracelet. "Look, this is Isaac's bracelet. He gave it to me as a token of his trust, of his confidence that I would honour his request. I will give the bracelet to you if you help me find the buried object."

With Henry's consent I began digging in the dirt with a metal spoon. It actually didn't take long at all before I found what I was looking for. "Holy shit, here it is!" I cried, and then apologized for my offensive language.

• • •

A man claiming to be an archaeologist was staying at a hotel on the north edge of the city near the forest reserve. He gave his name as Russell Adams, but almost nothing he said was true. He'd been at the hotel for several days, having all his meals there, rarely leaving his room.

But then he hired a driver to take him to a village near the animal sanctuary. It was a two-hour drive. He told the driver, "I'm only going to scope out the area. Just give me an hour there to get a sense of the place and then you can take me back to the hotel. What do you know about the place?"

The driver responded, "My people look down on that town. We say, 'If a fly lands on their food they will leave the food and eat the fly.' They are not bad or stupid people; they are just very poor and uneducated."

"I need someone who knows that area like the back of his hand."

"I know someone who is from that town. I can introduce you when we get back to the city. His name is Isaac."

When Adams was introduced to Isaac, he explained his proposition. "I'm looking for someone who knows the area around your home village. Specifically, I need someone familiar with the hills and caves in that area. I'll pay you well if you're able to help me."

Isaac accepted the assignment. He travelled with Adams to the village. On the way there, Adams explained in fuller detail what his mission was. Adams made his living finding ethnocultural artifacts and selling them to collectors. He explained that a lot of money could be made in this sort of business, so Isaac might find this a lucrative partnership. He had secured a copy of oral history interviews of the region and in these tapes a local man explained how elders of his village, fearing invasion from neighbouring tribes, had taken the precaution of hiding their most prized sacred item in a cave outside the village. Adams believed the artifact was still there and he needed Isaac's help in finding the cave.

Based on the description in the oral history, Isaac felt confident he knew where the cave could be found. He was uneasy, though, as traditional custom dictated that these sorts of relics had an integral relationship to the place of their origin and they were not to be removed from that land. In fact, it was believed that anyone removing a sacred item would be cursed.

They had their driver let them out in the village. From there, it took about an hour to walk on footpaths to where Isaac believed they would find the cave. Before long, they found a cave that matched the description in the notes Adams had taken from the oral history. They were able to enter the cave quite easily, but after about ten yards the floor of the cave dropped away, leaving a shaft of unknown depth. Isaac agreed to descend the shaft on a rope. It bottomed out after about twenty feet. Using a flashlight Isaac found a niche in the wall containing a small carving of a deer, which is the animal the locals believe was sent by god to look over them. He picked up the figurine and found that it was covered in a layer of moss but otherwise intact. He called up to Adams to report what he had found and then shinnied up the rope.

While Adams celebrated the discovery, Isaac felt a deep sadness.

By the time they finished walking back to the village, it was beginning to grow dark. They found the driver and Adams ordered him to take them back to the city without delay. He didn't feel safe being out at night.

Halfway back to the city, they were stopped by a man in a military uniform carrying a gun. Adams was immediately suspicious that the man was a bandit, not anyone there in an official, legal capacity. The man asked where they had been and where they were going. He then claimed the government had implemented an ID check and toll collection. He ordered everyone out of the vehicle. After Adams showed his ID, the man demanded an exorbitant amount of money as a road toll. Adams lost his cool and yelled, "This is ridiculous! You're nothing but a common bandit. We're not paying anything and we'll be reporting you to the police. Give me my ID back."

"You'll get your ID when you pay me," the man countered.

Adams lunged at him to grab the ID card from his hands. The bandit knocked him to the ground by striking his head with the butt of his rifle. He then shot Adams in the stomach, grabbed his wallet, and disappeared in his Jeep.

Isaac and the driver lifted Adams into the backseat of the vehicle. It looked unlikely that Adams would survive. Isaac removed the figurine from Adams's satchel, thinking the curse had claimed one life already and he had to get it back to the cave at the first opportunity. At the moment, however, the priority was to get Adams to the hospital in the city.

• • •

"I am pleased and honoured to be speaking to you this morning. My background is in anthropology and I have been working in the region for the last two years. My area of interest is the relationship between people and place, and how that connection impacts community well-being. I will be reporting on interviews I have conducted, primarily with elders, dealing with traditional knowledge and tribal religious beliefs. At the same time I am also a professional photographer and I'll be sharing some of my images with you throughout the talk."

I was pleased with how my talk went. People seemed engaged and the Q&A afterward was quite lively. One of the attendees questioned my academic rigour but otherwise the comments were positive.

As I was leaving the hotel, I encountered a young man who introduced himself as Isaac. He said he had heard I was someone who advocated for local heritage and said he needed to speak to me. He told me of an ancestral artifact that had been stolen and needed to be returned. I told him I would do whatever I could to help. He told me one man had been killed already and he feared for his own life. He also said he had buried the figurine in the dirt floor of his home. He said, "If anything happens to me, please contact my brother. He will tell you how to find my home. The item must be returned or my tribe will be plagued with misfortune. My brother teaches at the vocational training college. You can contact him there."

We made a plan to meet that Saturday to take the artifact back to its home. But he repeated, "If anything happens to me, you must do it without my help." I assured him I would. He gave me his bracelet as a form of pledge between us.

We said goodbye to each other and I watched him walk up the road. As he passed the gas station on the corner there was a huge explosion. I later learned that six people were killed, including Isaac.

RUB

I take the elevator to the eleventh floor. When the doors open, I look for a helpful sign saying something like, "1100-1149 to the left; 1150-1199 to the right." But there is nothing like that. I take a few tentative steps in one direction and conclude it must be the other way. But I soon realize that this is a more complex layout than rooms to the left and rooms to the right. Hallways branch off in different directions and the numbers seem to be clustered in random sequences. I find 1102 and think I must be getting warm but then the next room is 1180. I keep up my search for 1104D, getting more confused and anxious with each turn down a different hallway, never quite sure whether I have already been down that hallway or not.

I finally find 1104D and knock on the door. A gruff voice orders me to let myself in. A heavyset man is seated at a small table. He stares at me for the better part of a minute before barking at me. "What's your name? Show me some ID."

I pull out my driver's license and wait while he examines it. Then he hands it back to me without looking up. He also hands me an envelope. Having confirmed my identity he seems to have lost what little interest he had in me. He calls out, "Tam Yee!"

An Asian girl enters through a door I hadn't noticed. She looks like she might be sixteen. She steps tentatively into the room, closes the door behind her, and looks down like she is accustomed to being told what to do.

The man behind the desk speaks to me, again without looking up. "Everything you need is in the envelope. The address is in Newmarket. Paul is expecting you to report back by midnight. There's also a bit of cash for gas and food. Get her something to eat. She hasn't eaten since yesterday. Paul will take care of everything else after you drop her off. Enjoy your life in America, Tam Yee."

Tam Yee has only a small bag, what you might call an overnight bag, so she doesn't seem to mind carrying it while we search the halls for the elevator. We ride down together in an awkward silence. In the parking lot, I finally speak to her. I point across the lot and say, "The red Mazda, that's my car."

With her attention diverted, Tam Yee turns an ankle and stumbles to one knee. I help her up and ask if she is OK. She says, "Yes, I'm sorry." It is the first time I hear her voice.

"That man said you haven't eaten. You must be starving. The first thing we'll do is find somewhere nearby where you can have something to eat. Is there anything you'd prefer?"

"No, I would eat anything. Thank you."

I do a search on my phone and find a place called Diana's Bar and Grill just a few blocks away. It turns out to be better than I expected. The menu has a lot of the deep-fried food that is so ubiquitous, but, surprisingly, it also has a Korean page. I order bulgogi and Tam Yee orders bibimbap.

I feel tentative about making conversation with Tam Yee. It is tacitly understood that I have an assignment to carry out and the less I know beyond that, the better it will be for everyone. But the silence is becoming awkward so I start making small talk. "There used to be a lot of Korean restaurants near Bloor and Christie in Toronto. Not so much anymore. Neighbourhoods evolve. Last time I was there I only saw a few of them. How is your bibimbap?"

She looks me in the eyes for the first time and replies, "It's good. Thanks." And then she asks, "You like Korean food?"

"I love Korean food. I don't get to have it very often but whenever I get the chance I'm always happy. I love how the meal comes with kimchee and all the other condiments."

"I'm glad to hear you like it. You should visit Korea someday."

Before I have a chance to stop myself I venture into more personal territory. "Are you from Korea, Tam Yee?"

"Yes, I grew up in Chuncheon. It's about an hour from Seoul. And about an hour from the border with North Korea."

Although I have many questions I want to ask, I think better of it. It seems rude but I leave her information hanging there and focus on my meal.

When Tam Yee is done eating, I say, "Well, we really should be going. It will take us about four hours to get there."

Darkness has descended while we've been in the restaurant. We drive in silence out to Highway 9 and into the Greenbelt. There are no other cars on the four-lane highway when, for no reason I am aware of, I move from the right lane into the left lane. Almost as soon as I do that, I see a deer standing in the lane I've just vacated. My heart leaps in my chest. "My God, if I'd stayed in that lane we would have struck that deer! We could have been killed."

"Had you seen the animal before you changed lanes?" Tam Yee asks.

"No, that's the thing. I don't know why I moved over. I really don't know."

Something about the near accident jars me out of any reticence with Tam Yee. I ask her how she came to be in Canada.

"My uncle arranged for me to get a student visa. He coordinated things with this man, Paul. Paul Dane. I think he is your boss?"

I confirm that I work for Paul. Then I ask her, "So you're going to enroll in university? What will you study?"

"Paul hasn't told you anything? No, I am not allowed to go to school. That was only a way to get me into Canada."

"So, if you're not going to school, what are you going to do?"

Tam Yee looks over at me as if to detect whether to take my question seriously, whether I am as oblivious as I seem to be. But, of course, we are in a dark car so I don't know what she expects to discern.

"Are you aware of what Paul's business is?" she asks me.

"Oh, I think he's involved in a lot of things. He does some import/export business with Ukraine and Cuba, I believe. I think he deals in real estate. But, no, to be honest, I just do what I'm told and I don't ask a lot of questions. I think that's why Paul keeps me around."

"OK. Well, I guess you could say that I'm one of his investments."

"What do you mean?"

"Are you sure you want to hear this?"

I assure her I do but she sits silent for a while. I have to ask again. Then she begins to talk.

"A young woman has economic value. That is true in Korea. It is true in Canada. I think it is true everywhere. While I am a young, I am of interest to people like my uncle and your boss, Paul. My uncle really gave me no choice. He was my legal guardian and I was a burden. He convinced me that coming to Canada would open up opportunities but I would have to start out with work that he described as 'rub and tug.' He trained me himself so I would know what to do. Then he arranged things with Paul. I am not happy, but it is a place to start. I am told I can make good money at this work. I can send money to my sister back in Chuncheon. She is alone with three children. Eventually, I will get a real job. Maybe I can bring her here to live with me."

"Tam Yee, you said your uncle trained you. What do you mean?"

"I had no experience with sex. He got me to practise on him. Maybe it sounds shocking but it's what my sister and I grew accustomed to ever since our parents died and we went to live with him. He was not a good man."

My heart turns to a heavy, hollow beat like a bass drum. I don't know if I am more sad or angry.

"And you're OK with this 'bump and pull' thing?"

Tam Yee laughs. "It's called 'rub and tug.' And, no, I'm not OK with it, but what choice do I have?"

"Life doesn't have to be like this, Tam Yee." I'm not sure what I mean by this. I need some time to think, so we fall back into silence for a while.

Some thirty minutes later, I spot a familiar building at an intersection. I pull into the parking lot and put the car in neutral.

"Tam Yee, I've had an idea. My parents have a cottage on the Bruce Peninsula. There's no one there at this time of year, but they keep a key hidden in a shed out back. I could take you there and we could stay there as long as we like. We could come up with a better plan for your future. You don't want to do the 'bump and rub.' You don't want to work for Paul. What do you say?"

"Why would you do that? Paul will be furious with you."

I tell her something I hadn't known until I say it. "I'm done with Paul. I need to start building for a better future."

Tam Yee is silent for a minute and then says, "I'm scared, but I can't say no."

I don't wait for her to reconsider. I turn west toward the Bruce. Despite the risk we are both taking, the mood in the car lightens considerably. I start telling her about the cottage.

"I remember when my parents were first building the cottage. They bought beams from an old barn that was being torn down. My mom designed the cottage and I think she did a great job. It's right on the water and the wrap-around porch gives you a wonderful view. At that time, there were no other cottages nearby. Since then the area has seen a lot of development, but it's still pretty private. You'll love it."

Not hearing a reaction I glance over at Tam Yee, but she has dozed off. She sleeps until we arrive at the cottage.

I stop the car next to the cottage and then touch Tam Yee's arm to wake her up. I tell her to wait while I retrieve the key.

As would be expected the cottage is stuffy from being closed up since Labour Day, so I open some windows. Tam Yee doesn't seem fully awake so I invite her to use the bed in the room where my parents usually sleep.

"I'm afraid we don't have any linens, but there are plenty of blankets and comforters. Also, we have no groceries, of course, but there's a country store up the road where we can buy some essentials tomorrow."

The next morning I find Tam Yee sitting on the porch looking out over the lake.

"You were right. It is beautiful here. Very peaceful."

"I'm so glad you like it. I think my parents have some coffee beans in the pantry. You wait here while I put a pot on."

Before making coffee, I check my phone and find that Paul has called six times. What did I expect? I start to feel anxious but then I think of something that puts me into a panic. I immediately rush back out to the porch.

"Tam Yee, I'm such a fool. My phone was provided by Paul. I'm sure he has a tracker on it. It's only a matter of time before he follows us here. I think we have to leave. I'm not sure what to do."

Just then we hear a car pulling up on the gravel in front of the cottage. Tam Yee urges me to flee into the surrounding bush. "I will be fine. He won't hurt me. I have economic value."

Printed in the USA
CPSIA information can be obtained
at www.ICGtesting.com
JSHW021909020823
45659JS00005B/14